SCOTT GESCHWENTNER

MW01245388

MY ODYSSEY THROUGH A SUICIDE

WANDERING BY WAY OF A SATANIC ATTACK

outskirts
press

My Odyssey Through a Suicide
Wandering by Way of a Satanic Attack
All Rights Reserved.
Copyright © 2021 Scott Geschwentner
v4.0

The opinions expressed in this manuscript are solely the opinions of the author and do not represent the opinions or thoughts of the publisher. The author has represented and warranted full ownership and/or legal right to publish all the materials in this book.

This book may not be reproduced, transmitted, or stored in whole or in part by any means, including graphic, electronic, or mechanical without the express written consent of the publisher except in the case of brief quotations embodied in critical articles and reviews.

Outskirts Press, Inc.
http://www.outskirtspress.com

ISBN: 978-1-9772-4025-5

Cover Photo © 2021 www.gettyimages.com. All rights reserved - used with permission.

Outskirts Press and the "OP" logo are trademarks belonging to Outskirts Press, Inc.

PRINTED IN THE UNITED STATES OF AMERICA

A NOTE FROM ME TO YOU

I have high hopes that the title of this book left you with enough of a curiosity to read this story. I want you to know that I've made several references to the Holy Bible and I also made statements about God and the enemy, Satan, that relate to my journey. Most of these statements do not have a cited reference to support what was said, so I think it is important that I share my background with you. My background, however, doesn't make me an expert either, so I strongly encourage you to read this with an open mind and heart. And maybe my story will give you cause to read the Holy Bible personally, if you never have had this chance.

I grew up in the church and I spent time as a teenager in youth groups and church socials. Ministers I met along life's way encouraged me to read and understand the Bible, and I spent years as a young adult attending church retreats where we studied passages from the Bible, mainly the New Testament. I believe the statements I've made are true based on what I've learned over the years, so I am trusting that you will read these sections with an open mind, accepting them only as my honest opinion.

God has commissioned us to spread the word of the Bible, this is the meaning for the chosen in the Gospel, and it's important that we try to spread the good news when we are given the opportunity. I've chosen to write this book in hopes of giving God His glory for the blessings He has given to me in my life. If a person is wicked and full of sin, then we are called to warn him of his actions or God may hold us accountable. I've never found this to be easy, so I'm counting on the fact that by writing about it, I also will have the courage to do this as well.

Spiritual faith is the mystery of God that is beyond us, it is certainly not my intention to come to you with carnal faith. My hope is that if you've experienced having been attacked by Satan, but maybe not knowing he was the source, that your heart and mind will someday heal and become stronger. With God on our side, we can and will defeat the enemy. If you are like me, you may not have known you were being attacked, so this story might shed some light on something personal for you. I know there are people out there with stories much worse than mine, but I hope that my story somehow helps a little so you know that you are not alone regarding what you have experienced and that what happened was not just bad luck! Then hopefully we can rest in understanding our question of why God allowed this?

I also want to note that the Corona virus pandemic was starting to ramp up around the time that much of this was happening in my life. The isolation that came with the virus most likely did not help with matters, and this also caused many rather confused feelings as to whether this was the right time to pursue the course I had decided to take. Many of us were lucky enough to be working from home; ironically, it's the time I was actually wishing I could go in to work. At any rate, these uncertain times made me think of a time when cell phones became popular, many of us would actually turn the car around if we had left it at home. Of course, we are more likely to forget our keys rather than our phone, and now we need to turn the car around again in order to go get the mask that we left at home. So, that's life and we each choose how we want to live it!

I wish you God speed...

The Footprints
Poem and Prayer

One night I had a dream…

I dreamed I was walking along the beach with the Lord, and across the sky flashed scenes from my life. For each scene I noticed two sets of footprints in the sand; one belonged to me, and the other to the Lord. When the last scene of my life flashed before us, I looked back at the footprints in the sand. I noticed that many times along the path of my life, there was only one set of footprints.

I also noticed that it happened at the very lowest and saddest times in my life. This really bothered me, and I questioned the Lord about it. "Lord, you said that once I decided to follow you, you would walk with me all the way; but I have noticed that during the most troublesome times in my life, there is only one set of footprints. I don't understand why in times when I needed you the most, you should leave me."

The Lord replied, "My precious, precious child. I love you, and I would never, never leave you during your times of trial and suffering. When you saw only one set of footprints, it was then that I carried you."

Author Unknown

TABLE OF CONTENTS

Chapter 1

YOUR MIND IS a battlefield for Satan, and he uses it as a playground. Everyone has experienced, and most of us have lived through, some very trying and painful moments in our lives. My hope and prayer is that I will someday be able to listen to your story, because a part of me feels some of what you went through in your struggle.

I would like to tell you my story for a reason. I worry that many of us have the mindset that we can handle these troubling times on our own, that is to say without God. I want to say, we can't! Many years ago, I read this prayer, (or some refer to it as a poem), 'footprints in the sand' that was included at the beginning of this book. I was in high school at the time, and thanks to my parents, I did know who Jesus was. Still, this message was very comforting in some way. Oh, like most teenagers I had hardships, or at least I thought I did. I grew up with alcoholism and parents who separated, but I have heard the stories of others who experienced much worse. If you have read this poem then you most likely know from first-hand experience that someone at one time or another carried you through some very tough times. I pray that you know who the Person is in this prayer.

At the beginning of the year, I decided to end the marriage that I was in. Little did I know what I was about to experience in the coming months! Divorce is not easy; you've all most likely heard this from anyone who has dealt with it, or maybe you have been unfortunate enough to have experienced it firsthand. I can attest to the fact that the process can be long and exhausting, and even for the person who wants the separation; our inner self seems to always question our decision. Maybe I should have tried harder, maybe I shouldn't have given up, and maybe I should have read every self-help book out there in print that would give me the answer I was looking for. But my gut, that little inner voice in my head, told me that I didn't listen to and ask God in the first place. I'm not sure if most who go through a divorce can pinpoint one event that caused them to give up. I want to say that it seems there are a lot of people out there that just figure their relationship has run its course and since the romance is gone, and maybe the kids are out of the house, that maybe it's just time to move on without each other. I look at the events in my marriage, and when I look deep into myself, I believe with all my heart that if I had truly asked God if I should have entered into this marriage, He would have told me no. Sometimes God uses others in order to send His Word for us to hear, and I believe if I'd tried to understand the hesitancy that my children were sensing about this marriage, maybe I would have seen that God was talking through them. God has

His way of getting our attention, and sometimes we are just too hard-headed to listen to Him, but I am certain I wouldn't be living with the consequences of my actions now, if I listened in the first place. This is what happens, in my honest opinion, when we don't stop and listen to God. We get ourselves in trouble. But I also believe Jesus is there to pull us out every time--that is, if we ask Him.

I would ask that you look back on your own life and see how many times you've witnessed only that one set of footprints in the sand. For me this past year, those footprints in the sand saved my life from the powerful grips of the devil. I feel so strongly about my story that I believe I need to warn you to be careful! Satan is a master of deception and is a master liar, and his timing is perfect because he knows exactly when you are most vulnerable to his attacks. Satan has successfully deceived the whole world, Revelation 12:9. God has given him this power on earth, why? I don't really know.

But God still has overarching authority, this I do know! This authority over the evil on earth is real, Satan is real, and we need to know that we can reject Satan's suggestions. I don't want to claim that I am an authority; this is just what I have learned and experienced over the years from others who have studied the Bible. So why am I telling you this? I am hoping that by hearing my story, you will become aware of Satan's little tricks. They are often little things that trip us up and steer us away from God. It is this information that is important to the story that I want to share with you.

The divorce was frustrating, to say the least. Both of us had been married before, and although my previous divorce involved children, this one was setting up to be an even longer exhausting journey. Our relationship had dwindled to the point in which we no longer were even acknowledging each other's birthdays, or celebrating our anniversary, much less celebrating Christmas together. I found myself taking vacations with my kids, because I sure didn't want to spend that time with her. She spent a lot of her time away as well, doing whatever she was doing, and I really didn't care anymore. The lies and deception that I caught her in left me with an angry spirit, and I know I voiced the words of forgiveness, but now I know my heart wasn't in it, and I have to think it probably wasn't to God's satisfaction either. Not only that, but I also know that I wasn't willing or able to let go of it either, and do the other part of forgiving, which is forgetting.

Things hadn't started that way, though. If it had, I'm sure the marriage would have never gone forward. I can only say this because I've known couples that start a relationship out this way, and for whatever reason, continue the relationship. There were a few red flags, and I was aware of these, but life has a way of playing tricks on you. I was struggling with myself, wondering if I was being too judgmental, or was I writing someone off before really giving them a chance? I believe I was at a point in my life when I questioned my own behavior. At any point, I found myself working really hard to overcome these feelings that had unfortunately turned out to be valid. But let's back up a bit and start over from the beginning.

The story of how we met was one of those fun moments in life, usually a crowd pleaser, as the saying goes. We were both part of a singles group that would gather together for some activity. The night I met her; the activity happened to be country dancing. Before that night, I had never seen her at any of the other activities I attended, and to make things more interesting, I was actually supposed to be meeting someone else there that evening. This story doesn't seem to have the same appeal writing about it as opposed to telling it in person, but the girl that I was supposed to meet there had some problem at home and so she never made it.

I happened to be sitting right behind this person, who was to become my future wife, without even knowing it. I'd been listening to the guy next to me ramble on about how he wanted to ask her to dance, but apparently didn't have the nerve or whatever was needed to get him off of his chair. I even sat there giving this guy words of encouragement so he would get up and go ask her. Then to his dismay, his opportunity vanished when a song came on that I wanted to dance to, so I leaned forward, tapped her on the shoulder, and pointed to the dance floor. She nodded yes, and from there, we spent the rest of the evening dancing, sitting at a little table for two and talking to each other all the way into the wee morning hours when the bar closed.

It was summer when we met, and one of the activities we decided to do together as a group was to go water skiing. When I was younger, I bought a boat, and well, it was pretty much a piece of junk, but I wanted a ski boat. So this old boat became my project, and anyway, I wasn't doing anything with the other nine projects I had going on at the time.

So I started out refurbishing the old boat by first overhauling the outboard motor, then I replaced the outdoor carpeting and installed new back-to-back folding seats. From there I proceeded building a bench across the back with storage underneath, and then I added some new instruments on the dashboard. Once that was done, I did my best in order to polish the hull, and then to finish it off, I added some cool stickers. And well when I was all finished, it still was pretty much a piece of junk. But it was a great ski boat and it was mine. The motor wasn't quite powerful enough to easily pull a slalom skier out of the water, so we had to become experts at getting up on the skis, but once we were up, that old boat could really glide through the waves. And even though it had been years since I 'renovated' that boat, I guess I'd surprised her, and myself for that matter, at how well I remembered the art of waterskiing. Apparently, she was very competitive because I found out later that she was taking off of work in order to go skiing without me, just so she could get better. Now, I'm not really suggesting that competition is a bad thing; I certainly have this in my blood. But as I got to know this person, I was getting the feeling she just wasn't that happy with what she'd accomplished in her life, and often it felt as though she was trying to prove something to me. This might have been the first flag?

The water-skiing activity was the last time that we participated in a group, so when winter rolled around, we found ourselves atop the snowy mountains of Colorado. Though I had never taken lessons, I had been skiing for years and I guess I just figured out what worked for me along the way. Skiing with her started out fun, and even though she took lessons before I met her, she often seemed discouraged just because she wasn't able to keep up with me at times. I remember giving her suggestions and pointers along the way when she would ask for my advice, but sometimes my way of doing things didn't match up with what her instructor told her to do, so this often created a lot of confusion and frustration for her.

Years ago when I took my kids up skiing, they didn't seem interested in taking lessons with the other kids, so they learned to ski my way. Nowadays, they can both out-ski me, so I usually try to find an excuse to have a beer on the ski lodge deck, but it may have something to do with me being an old guy now. Anyway, one day I saw they had been getting pretty good on the blue slopes, so I tricked them and took a turn down a black run. When we got to the bottom of the run, I commented how well they skied it and then informed them they had just done a black run. After the initial surprise and shock wore off, they lowered their weapons pointed at me and decided that was pretty cool, so we ended up doing the run again.

It had been my philosophy that you won't get better unless you push yourself, but when I tried doing the same thing with the wife, things didn't end as well. I had taken her down a double diamond that I was pretty sure she could handle, but even though she struggled a bit, she made it down just fine. All along she had been complaining that I wasn't telling her something because she felt she still wasn't able to keep up with me. But although I tried to tell her she had made it down a double diamond, she didn't like the idea of being tricked. I suppose I get that, but often many of us won't do something because of fear, and I know she would never have gone down that run if she knew what it was before she did it. So not knowing how to handle this, skiing with her became more of a chore. Somehow, she continued to think I was leaving out that one ingredient that would have made her an expert skier.

Okay, maybe these were red flags, or maybe some are saying there's nothing wrong with wanting to improve oneself. I guess, in my opinion, the line gets crossed when the competitiveness reaches a point that you're not being honest with the other person. Mostly, I think I was just trying to figure out what I missed in the relationship. But then there were the times that we spent together that were extremely enjoyable, like the traveling we did. She was originally from Europe, but she had seen more of the states than I had, and I was raised in the states. Guess the other old saying goes, you don't spend time in your own backyard? Or something like that. Well, we flew to the West Coast and enjoyed wine country, and we flew to the East Coast and ate lobster. All in all, these were pretty fun trips, but how can you not have fun when you're full of wine? It seems odd and sad to me that something can start out rather nice, but life has a way of changing things.

Then one day, while avoiding the coasts, we found ourselves in the middle of Arizona where I asked her to marry me. The question had entered my mind minutes before I asked her and I knew if I didn't say something soon, the words would never come. So, as we both were sitting there in shock, I was thinking to myself, did I really say that, and she wasn't too convinced either because her response was 'are you being serious'? Well, this certainly sounds like a good way to start things.

But anyway, when we returned to Colorado, we decided to just

SCOTT GESCHWENTNER

have a nice private little ceremony. The wedding day was memorable; we sought the services of a minister in the Colorado Rockies. The previous day had left a blanket of snow on the ground, and the sun was shining in a cloudless sky the day of the ceremony. That evening we found ourselves in Steamboat enjoying the bubbles in the hot tub and even more the bubbles that seem to come in the Champagne bottles. From there we started our lives together.

So, fast forwarding, when I approached her that fateful day, I told her that it seemed obvious neither one of us were interested in saving the marriage, so I said I was going to file for the divorce. She had no reply; in fact she didn't even look at me while I was talking to her. I remember standing there for a while, but she just continued doing what she was doing and acting like I wasn't even there. So, I met with an attorney and discussed my intentions in the days following. I was hoping that we could go through mediation and come to an agreement on our own, while keeping the courts and lawyers to a minimum, but this hope quickly disappeared. After my first meeting with the attorney, I made the appointment at a time I knew my then-wife would be free for the both of us to attend mediation.

Of course, when that day came, she was nowhere to be found, so I decided to file on my own. In the weeks following, the papers came so I set them on the kitchen counter, but they continued to be ignored. I found myself placing the papers next to her purse on the counter, then in front of her coffee pot, and finally hiding her keys under the papers, but after about another week of playing these games, I realized she was not going to reply. So, I let her know that if she wasn't going to acknowledge the papers, I would be forced to have her served. I would have thought she'd do something at this point because who in their right mind wants to be served? This was how the process had started, so it is probably fairly clear how uncomfortable my situation had become. When the server showed up on a Sunday afternoon at the house, my hopes of having this sort of thing done at her work quickly vanished. I answered the door and let her know there was someone there that wanted to see her. She must have known who it was because she wouldn't go to the front door, so I was left with the decision to have the guy come in and give them to her. Of course, she picked this time to let loose her tongue with the guy serving the papers, so an already uncomfortable situation turned quickly into an extremely hold-your-breath type circumstance. I just couldn't understand what she was doing.

We hadn't had a meaningful conversation in over a year, why would she even want to be holding onto this? I started trying to figure it out on my own, since she refused to tell me anything. I assumed she just wanted to stay in the house and live out her life the way things were. I sure didn't want to live this way any longer, it seemed like a waste of two lives to me. So, if I'm correct in assuming that God didn't want this union between us, does that mean Satan had a victory? Maybe, but this is what he does, or at least that's what he tries to do: create friction and doubt between people, and he's pretty good at doing this. I believe he tries to do this whether it's between two people or if it's between two countries. That is what he is about, and that is all he is about, creating divisions.

And I thought the serving of the papers would do the trick,

SCOTT GESCHWENTNER

maybe she would decide to play along or at least realize she was making a bad situation into a horrible nightmare. A bad choice of words for what was going on, but the time had come and gone and still she indicated no response, so the judge finally made a decision to enter a judgment of default against her. With all that was happening, the frustration and confusion was unknowingly building inside me to the point when anger was taking over again.

Now, close to two months had gone by, and I wasn't the only one baffled and upset by what was going on, my lawyer told me in the 20 years she had been handling divorces, she had never seen anything like this. I inquired a couple times as to what she was doing, and at one point I accused her of using me just so she could continue to live in the house and raise her garden. To my surprise, I learned later that this accusation wasn't that far off. However, there was only one time that she finally responded to me and her words were 'get the (insert a really bad word here) out of my sight'. So again, if she hated me that much, why didn't she want this divorce?

So, a couple more months went by along with a couple more unanswered motions against her. I believe the judge had had enough at this point, so after over five months of dealing with this, the court entered in a final divorce decree. Since she wouldn't respond, the court went with my suggested financial split and why not? No one was contesting it. And looking back, I think I was too generous. This of course was my opinion, as the guy talking here, but to support this, my attorney agreed that I was giving her too much also. I just wanted out at the time, and I didn't want to be fighting about the money. I had also decided to give her extra, so that I wouldn't be held responsible for monthly payments to her. After my last divorce where children were involved, I was committed to paying a chunk of my paycheck to the ex for almost 16 years and that just seemed like forever back then. Once that had finally come to an end, the last thing I wanted now was to be stuck in monthly payments again to someone I didn't think even deserved it. So, here we were, the divorce was final and the judge ordered us to sell the house we both were still living in and split the proceeds per the agreement, the one I made.

Now for probably most of us, this next part of the story may be disturbing. It was terribly disturbing for me. You see, from here this story doesn't have a happy ending because as the title suggests—it actually ends in suicide. This word was always a hard concept for me to hear, and now it is even harder, but if this word is hard for you, as much as I would like for you to know my story, the mental image may be extremely unsettling.

When the divorce was final and the house that we were living in was sold, the months of waiting had come to an end, and her stalling tactics had also come to an end, a complete end. To back up just a little, from the time that I started the process, I shared with you how my then wife decided to ignore everything. Maybe this was her way of dealing with what was happening and in turn stalling what was going to happen. I had the unpleasantness of serving her, filing motion after motion due to her unresponsiveness, and even having to file contempt of court, which had been prompted by the judge at the time. She refused to do anything or say anything. It may seem callous, but when you have been lied to and deceived, your actions are

SCOTT GESCHWENTNER

not often coming from a good place, and I was not in a good place. I was deeply hurt, and I wanted the pain to go away, and I'm sure she may have been in pain too, but her silence had built a big wall between us at this point and I had no desire to knock it down. I may have the sympathy and understanding from some, but others may fault me in some way. I only know that I was in a very dark place.

Chapter 2

WHAT HAPPENED NEXT will be with me forever. I've been hoping that by writing about it some things may become clearer to me. Maybe you've tried this, writing a letter to someone that you've never intended to send just so you can organize your thoughts? In truth, this is how the book got its start but I have omitted pages of thoughts I meant only for her, once it began to develop. I know a part of me wants the whole story out on the table, but another part of me is also terrified to find out the real truth. Maybe, things are better left alone, as the old saying goes, but something in me wasn't going to let go of this.

Of the several things that had already come to light, much of it was a pretty good blow to the old self esteem. Somehow, for some reason, I still found I was torturing myself to learn as much of the truth as possible, even though it would mean feeling even more depressed. So here I was, the day of closing had arrived, and as I stated earlier, the final days of silence had also come to an end.

Now her stalling tactics were at the end of the line. If she continued down this path, it would only mean disaster and most of that would be directed toward her. Well, turns out that is exactly the reality for the both of us that day. She had not shown up at the signing, and rage and anger took complete control over me. Upon finding out, I left work steaming and headed home. The drive was uncomfortably long; I couldn't actually believe this was really happening. When I finally arrived at the house, I was trying to compose myself but the anger in me wanted to know why this was happening. Then, as I entered the house, I discovered the answer I had never expected. The bedroom door had been barricaded, but without having the understanding as to why, I leaned on the door in order to open it. I originally thought how strange it was that the door was closed, but then I finally forced it open far enough so I could stick my head through a small opening. I then stood there in disbelief as I looked at her positioned in the middle of the bedroom. She was just sitting there on a chair that had been given to me when I was a kid. She had been facing her computer, which was open in front of her, and on the screen were videos playing from our wedding day. She had put on her wedding dress and wedding sandals, and in her hand, she was clinching a 9mm handgun that was sitting on her lap. Looking up, I saw the blood down the side of her cheek and down the side of her dress that had been facing opposite the door. Her lips were tightly pushed together, and her eyes seemed to be tightly shut. As I stood there in a total loss of control, the anger I had been feeding earlier turned into something else and I just stopped.

My life had changed forever. I did not see the signs, and I couldn't see past my own pain. For weeks after seeing her in the room, I could not stop asking why. The image of her sitting there would wake me at night, and I just played the scene in my head over and over as if I had been there in the room. I couldn't stop imagining what she must have been doing leading up to the time just before she decided to pull that trigger. Was she terrified at the act she was about to do, or was she in some peaceful hallucinated state of mind knowing the end was near? Questions followed more questions, and knowing I would never have the true answers was even more daunting. I couldn't sleep, I was unable to function at work, I would go days without eating, and the unbelievable feeling of loneliness and despair completely consumed me. My entire world was collapsing around me, and I felt like I had been thrown into a deep dark tunnel with no way out. Was she hoping to turn my life upside down? She had left me nothing, nothing except a mess to clean up and an image that I would face for the rest of my life.

And this is when Satan became deeply interested and involved in my life! I asked the question earlier if Satan had had a victory by splitting us apart. God is all good, so it didn't seem to make sense that God would split us up, but on the other hand, if it was not His will that we were together, then maybe we had just missed out on His blessing of being and staying together? But when she pulled the trigger that day, did Satan have another victory? I hate to think that he did. Satan managed to separate her from family and from friends, which must have left her with such a desperate feeling of loneliness.

SCOTT GESCHWENTNER

I had often talked about Jesus with her, and based on her questions I know she was interested in what I had to say, but I'm now wondering if I did and said things in the right way. She obviously felt that she had no one left, and maybe she hadn't realized Jesus was there ready to carry her through another trial. But this is where my understanding becomes somewhat clouded. I have experienced some dark places in my life, but something in me has always told me that sooner or later things will get better. And although the better part sometimes took years, I always knew someday I would see the light. But knowing that there was someone out there who seemed to be feeling that all hope was gone forever and there could never be happiness again was very frightening to me. Why God would allow Satan to get such a hold on her is frustrating, but God's plan is perfect. I just hope to have the understanding someday.

I think you know that feeling when you have to grab your neck so you can suck another breath in? This was the feeling I experienced next. All of that anger, all of the pain and frustration, the months I spent waiting for the court to make a decision, and not to mention the hate that built up in those months had all disappeared and this foreign emotion of compassion took complete control over me. We were already legally divorced, so I surely wasn't responsible for her now, but compassion or maybe it was the mercy from God that indwelled me because the next day I made the arrangements for her funeral.

Since I wasn't given the chance to say goodbye to her, given suicide decides that for you, I asked the funeral home director if I could see her one last time in order that I might have some closure. It was the day before her service; I sat alone with her in the funeral home praying that God would forgive her for what she had done to herself. I asked her to forgive me for the pain that I caused her, and then I told her I would forgive her for all the past pain that I had felt. I then got up, told her that I didn't want to say goodbye, but instead I just wanted to say see you later.

When the service was over, I took her remains down to the river where I loved to fly fish, and I spread her ashes out there. How strangely odd it was. I chose a spot where I wasn't likely to be disturbed by others that were there to enjoy the river so I could have this last moment in privacy. When I opened the urn, I discovered that her remains had been placed into a clear plastic bag. Since the neck of the urn was smaller than the base, kind of like the ship in the bottle mystery, what I hoped to be a special moment had turned into a desperate attempt to quickly remove her remains. Since I couldn't get the bag out, I found myself cutting the top open and spreading some of her ashes until I was able to pull the rest of the bag out of the urn. I'd never done this before so I really had no idea what to expect, and for reasons that later became clear to me, I was also expecting her remains to be dusty. I guess some of the thanks here goes to Hollywood, but the Bible also states that the Lord formed man of the dust and to dust we shall return, but her remains were more like salt crystals, which I think sort of makes sense. So, then I wanted to look up the definition of cremation just to see what Webster had to say about it, and the first definition I came across defined it as exposing the body to flame and intense heat followed by pulverization of bone fragments. Wow, is there anything about this story that isn't violent? So anyway, this whole process of scattering her ashes was taking a lot longer than I anticipated, which caused me concern that someone would be wandering by. I mean what would you say if someone came by: oh pardon me, I'm just spreading some ashes of my deceased ex, so could you give me a moment? I'm not trying to be disrespectful here, but sometimes I think we need to experience some of the comfort of that unexpected humor that comes out of a tragedy that occurs.

But this brings me back to my anger. Where did it go? What stopped fueling it and why was I even able to do something like this? I grew up around anger, but I don't want to go down that path and blame what happened in the past for how I'd been acting in the present. I know I had a conditioned anger. By that, I mean the angry person in me would always get the job done, so how could that not be a conditioned outcome to keep him around? If you've carried around anger, as I have for most of my life, I would encourage you to become familiar with the Book of Sirach. Sir 27:30, Wrath and anger are hateful things, yet the sinner hugs them tight. The vengeful will suffer the Lord's vengeance, for He remembers their sins in detail. I don't know about you, but that passage just scares the hell out of me. Remembers every detail? The passage goes on to say that you must forgive your neighbor's injustice, if you want to be forgiven for what you've done. Wow, would that be a clear enough message? I know how hard it has been for me to forgive, which is probably the reason I've carried around so much anger. The devil plays rough and dirty and his only goal is to destroy, so it stands to reason that we need an arsenal to defend ourselves. Hopefully, we can see our arsenal is the Word of God given to us in the Bible.

But to continue, I suppose this is where the story of me and my ex-wife more or less ends and my story begins. Of course, then life happens, and there is always that next 'but' that comes along, for me anyway! Now, I'm standing in a house where someone had just taken her life, and I'm looking around at the unspeakable mess that was left behind for me. I had already purchased a townhome just before the tragedy occurred, and now I'm worried about my job. With two mortgages, two water bills, two electric bills, and now feeling an overwhelming fear that nobody would ever want to buy a house where someone had just shot herself. So what was I supposed to do now? I surely didn't want to live in the house; I wasn't even comfortable being there during the day, I couldn't imagine how things would feel during the night. How was I going to get this fixed? Who was going to fix it, and oh, by the way, how much is this going to cost? I thought about ways to get out of the contract with the townhouse, but where would I go then? I must say, hopelessness and helplessness, two of my worst enemies had once again come back to me and were again settling in on my thoughts.

My eternal thank you goes out to the chaplain that came over to be with me that day. I vaguely remember someone asking me if I needed to talk to someone, but I don't even remember what I said. I do recall the chaplain asking if he could pick up the Bible that had been sitting on my nightstand, then he began reading me some passages. I was a mess; I couldn't stop thinking about what I just saw and the pain was mounting. He was talking to me because the detective that was there was trying to find out the events that occurred that day. I remember telling them that something was not feeling right all week.

20   SCOTT GESCHWENTNER

We were scheduled to move out the next day, and she had not packed a thing. I convinced myself that she was just going to load up her car and leave with whatever she could get in it.

The detective wanted to know why I came back that afternoon, so I was explaining that she hadn't shown up for the signing, so I drove to the house to find out why. I told him when I got to the house, I walked in and I left the front door wide open, which is something I'd never done before. I walked around the house and didn't see her, so I went to the bedroom. The door was shut and when I turned the handle, the door would not open. My first thought was that she was on the other side of the door holding it shut. So after some time of talking through the door and not getting a response, I put my shoulder to the door. She had barricaded the other side, but I was able to get it open just barely enough to stick my head through the door. I suppose it was enough of a shock seeing her sitting there in her wedding dress with the videos of our wedding day playing on her computer because I hadn't even noticed that she had shot herself.

I was asking her what she was doing and why had she'd blown off the signing. Then I asked her why she blocked the door, and as I started to say, do you realize the trouble...? but before I was able to finish that sentence, I noticed the gun in her lap. At that point a reflex caused me to jump back, thinking she was going to use it on me, and then something just seemed odd and that's when I stuck my head back in and saw the blood down the side of her face and on her dress. And as I looked further down, I saw the puddle of blood on the floor. I pushed harder on the door, but still couldn't get it open. Then again, I stopped and stared at her for a while, stared at the blood on the floor. Her hand looked to be tightly gripped on the gun that she was holding and meanwhile I was watching to see if her chest had moved so much as a whispered breath. After some time went by, it was then the reality of what had happened hit me and I just stepped back.

I started walking to the front door and I remember not really feeling anything at that point. Then I pulled my phone out of my pocket and called for emergency. Time seemed to stop; I don't remember hearing any sounds. I can't recall the time it took for police to arrive, but when the first officer came up to the door, I just looked at him and said she shot herself. When the sheriff got to the bedroom door, he gave it a push and then he backed up took a run at it and broke the door down. That's when I got the full view of the room and also the side of her that I couldn't see looking through the door. He looked at her sitting in the chair and then at the room. He turned toward me and quickly grabbed me by the arm and took me to the other side of the house. About that time, another officer arrived and I heard him shout "don't let him back over here." So, I spent the rest of that afternoon on the other side of the house walking to the bathroom, then through the garage into the back yard and then back again. It seemed every time I turned around, there was someone different entering the house. The chaplain had been walking with me, trying to give me space, but at the same time listening to me blubber on. I remember grabbing onto his coat and telling him to make sure and let me know when they were going to wheel her out. I kept telling him that I didn't want to see her being wheeled out, please, I don't want to see that!

SCOTT GESCHWENTNER

Chapter 3

Do you believe in ghosts? I needed a change of subject here in order to lighten things up for a moment, feeling the mind going into overload from the memory of that day. Anyway, I remember back when I was about seven years old. I was one of five kids in our family and the other four were all girls. Oh sure, now I have your sympathy! My mom had lost two others at birth, and I was told they were boys. Why they didn't make it is a question I hope to know one day, but that would have evened things out a bit for me. I remembered the day I found out this news, my twisted little mind thought it was probably me because I never could do anything right the first time, so three times was a charm, but I had never told anybody that until now.

Anyway, my parents had a small house on Gilpin Street, so I got to share a bedroom with one of my sisters. One night something woke me up. We each had our own twin bed and there was a little nightstand between them. Something had caught my eye on the floor, and when I looked down off the bed, there was a little girl playing this game called Jacks. Maybe if you were around in the 70s, you would know this game. The weird part of this story is that I don't remember anything after that, at least not until the next morning. My sister had been talking to my mom in the kitchen and was telling her about this little girl that she saw sitting between the beds. All of the sudden it occurred to me that I had witnessed the same thing. When we both gave our account as to what we saw, it was quite the back-of-the-neck hair-raising story. I never saw her again, but it's a clear image in my mind to this day. Could just be the imagination of some kids, but it sure seemed real to me at the time. So then of course, visiting ghost towns and staying at hotels that people claimed to be haunted became a real thrill for me. I've never seen anything, or anybody for that matter, but that hasn't stopped me from visiting other so-called haunted towns and hotels.

But walking back into the house the next day was probably one of the scariest moments of my life!

The restoration company had been to the house in order to clean up the 'biological' mess and they had also removed the soiled items from the previous day. I looked around the room, probably still in some state of shock, and replayed the events of the day before. I looked at the broken door leaning against the wall, the carpet and padding that had been cut out and a piece of the subfloor that had been removed. The window blinds had been torn off, and the smell of cleaner overwhelmed the entire house. I stared at the clothes hanging in the closet, the boxes of

SCOTT GESCHWENTNER

shoes stacked on the shelves and I started to wonder, what was it that I was supposed to do now? Looking around, I walked toward the window looking up at the wall. I ran my finger along the drywall and then into a hole. I thought, "Wow, that's about the size of a bullet." It just didn't seem real; I surely never expected to be dealing with this. I just couldn't believe she could take it this far, why anyone would feel the need to take it that far is still a question I haven't been able to stop asking myself.

The previous day had been a madhouse. Police were coming in and out; an ambulance crew along with the coroner was in the room, I guess doing what they had to do. The chaplain had told me that there was a news crew set up across the street with a camera pointed right at the house, I guess hoping for some juicy news to report. Being on this side of things, I sure have a different opinion about that now. How disgustingly rude it seemed. How I just wanted to ask the guy if he had any decency—any respect of others. Here I was dealing with a life-crushing event and this guy just wanted some ghastly gossip for the news.

It was sometime after I found her in the room the previous day that for some reason, I felt I needed to call my supervisor. I had left work rather unexpectedly, but I wasn't concerned that he was wondering where I was. He was a person of faith and we often talked about Jesus and the Bible, so I think a part of me was looking for some comforting words. I thought that I had pulled myself together at this point. As I paced around the house, I started dialing the phone. I was experiencing that numb feeling that some get from crying so hard for so long. But as soon as he answered, my throat swelled up and then locked and as hard as I tried to hold back, the emotions were a little too much for me. It must have been pretty hard to be on the other end of that phone call. I have often wondered what he was doing just before I called. I've never really wanted to ask him.

Growing up I was an incredible fan of the series MASH, and if you happened to be a fan also, you probably have some idea how this relates. At the beginning of each series, they would always play the theme song from the original movie, but they conveniently left out the words.

If you have ever read the words to this theme song, you would probably understand why. The first set of lyrics goes something like this, "Through early morning fog I see, visions of things to be, the pains that are withheld for me, I realize and I can see that suicide is painless."

For me, these words mean the aftermath of suicide is painless since the trials from this life are over. I really can't imagine that the act of firing a bullet into your head would be painless, but that's one I would choose not to ever experience first-hand. Unfortunately, there is a harsh reality in these words, and many people have chosen this path as their own. It is a sad thought that this would seem to be a choice, to end the life that God gave you. I know the feelings of depression, and I have had to take medications in the past to help me overcome it. The thought of actually taking my life had not entered my mind, but I'd experienced some extremely lonely times. I believe my faith would never have allowed me to actually go through with something so permanent anyway. I also would have dreaded the idea of standing before God and saying to Him that I had enough and I was tired of the life I had. I know that I have found myself yelling at God at times, asking how much more of this can I take? Sometimes things get better, sometimes we just need to live with the choices we've made by taking up our cross and carrying it, because those choices have come with consequences. It's a fact of life, but I don't think it's our choice to end it on our own, and this is the reason I've chosen to make statements about God and the Bible in this story, I hope and pray that one would turn to faith to overcome whatever obstacle has been put in front of them rather than giving up. This is the main reason for my story, faith has saved my life, and I wish it could have saved hers!

It would have been nice if I could insert a long pause here, but the story continues. The next day I got up, made my coffee and headed off to work. It wasn't until I sat down on the chair in my office that I said to myself, what in the hell am I doing here? I walked by the office where my supervisor was and just gave him a wave as I was walking out. I can't imagine what he was thinking. A friend and coworker was walking in the door just as I was walking out and he gave me a funny look. Then he said, "You look like you've been through it!" At that point it occurred to me that I'd just gotten out of bed that morning without showering and still wearing the same clothes I had on the day before. I started to tear up and then I told him my ex had shot herself the previous day.

It just floors me that my mouth had no filter on that day, and I severely shocked him judging from the expression on his face. I would hate to give this as a warning, next time you ask how someone is doing, think of the words I said first! So then, the next day my supervisor called me and asked if I would like to come by his house and have dinner. I hadn't answered the phone, because that was the day that I was headed to the funeral home to say goodbye, or as it turned out I just wanted to be with her so I could tell her: I'll see you later.

After I had sat with her and made my peace, I prayed for a while and then I got up. I was walking toward the door when the funeral director saw me and asked if I was doing okay. I remember looking at him probably just giving him a blank look while shaking my head and then I turned and went back into the room where she was lying. I did this three times before finally saying to him that everything was okay now, and I was okay, and I also figured I wasn't the first one to do this under the circumstances. Her pain was over and she was in God's hands now. When I got back in my car, I called my supervisor and told him I would really like the company. I remember the fear I felt when I first walked into the funeral home. Thinking of her lying there felt overwhelming, but once I was alone in the room with her, something just came over me. It was comforting to see her for some closure, to be able to tell her my thoughts without anger and fear driving my words and actions. And at this point, it really felt as though someone had put a shield around me, the tightness in my chest was completely gone, and I felt nothing but peace leaving there that day.

It's amazing to me what the human body can withstand. I was thinking back to when my dad passed away. He had smoked nearly all of his life, and from the stories, I imagined him as a baby finishing his milk and then grabbing a cigarette afterward.

I'm not too sure if he was able to roll his own back then but I guess you would have had to know my dad to understand that. As a kid, I used to watch him light a cigarette with the previous one that he was smoking. He always told me it saved matches. I hated the smoke though. We didn't know much about second hand smoke back then, but I would irritate the heck out of him when I rolled down the window in the truck when it was 10 below zero outside. The day that he died, my then-wife had called my pager. This was the day before cell phones, and she was pregnant with our second so I had this pager in case she needed to get in touch with me. Anyway, she beeped me, so when I called her back, she said my mom told her that I needed to get down to the hospital. Well, if you have ever read the book 'cry wolf' you probably know how I was feeling at that moment; because I think this was the fifth time that I had to hurry to the hospital. So, I finished what I was doing, not really in a hurry, and headed over to the hospital. As I walked down the hall my sister came up and grabbed me in order to hurry me along saying, "Dad is dying."

We turned the corner and walked into the room, and as I looked at my dad, I instantly knew something was very wrong. His face had turned yellow, and I watched his chest slowly rise up and it was difficult to even see it fall. He looked as if he was trying to open his eyes, but he couldn't. Then I looked over at my mom when she leaned in toward my dad and said, "Scott is here." I watched his chest as it went up one more time. Seconds later, my dad passed.

As I stood there in disbelief, I thought, "Did God have my dad hold on until I got there?" How selfish it was for me to not take that call seriously. If he had died before I arrived at the hospital, how would I have handled that, knowing I had taken my time to get there? Would I be carrying around grief or guilt and more regrets in my life? Maybe he asked God to wait until I got there because he knew what he had put me through in life. Maybe this was an answer from God for an unknown prayer?

He had come from a generation and background in which showing emotion was a weakness. I think he was so hard on me because that was what he thought he needed to do in order to make me strong. I recall a time when my sisters were fighting in the basement of the house, and I guess my dad had had enough, so when he came down to stop it; I was the one who got the belt. I had nothing to do with the fight; I remember just sitting on the couch watching them argue. Later, when my dad found out I wasn't the one fighting, I think he felt badly, but he never apologized to me for what happened. His way of apologizing to me that night was offering me a stick of gum.

I don't want to leave you with the impression that my dad was always like this; he was a good dad and provided for all of us pretty well. He always made us work for everything, but again, it was his generation and maybe that wasn't such a bad thing anyway. He was probably often treated similarly by his dad when he was a kid. As I sit here and recall some of the stories he told, things didn't sound that fun growing up back then. It was a cycle that many of us have tried to break when we reared our own family. Curiously, now that I'm writing about this, I know it wasn't okay to be fighting with my sisters, but I would often get into fights when I was in grade school. The older kids would often come over to our playground and steal our ball or

SCOTT GESCHWENTNER

make fun of my classmates. I was never one to stand for this, so my way of dealing with it was to start swinging. I can't even begin to count how many times I was hauled into the principal's office for fighting, but once my dad had me in the truck and out of the principal's office, he would always want to know if I was able to finish the fight. I guess this was showing him that I was tough, and I think some of his goals in life were meant to make me tough.

And it seems odd that I knew it wasn't okay for those older kids to be making fun of my classmates back then, since this was later referred to as bullying. After my former wife had passed, I starting reading every book on suicide I could find, and while reading one day I stumbled across a sad story of a teenager who decided to end their life because they were being bullied. ⸺

When I started high school, it had been a life-changing experience for me. I guess one kid figured out that I was an easy target. I was constantly being bullied and talked down to by this guy until one day I guess I had had enough. I was at my locker switching books for my next class when he came up behind me and starting talking his usual crap. Well, I placed all of my books into my locker then turned around and clocked him. He went flying back onto his butt and his books went flying all over the floor. The other students all backed up, I suppose waiting to see what was going to happen next, and just as I went toward him, my French teacher grabbed my arm and pulled me aside. I was able to stand up for myself and vent that day, and it being the 1970s, I really didn't get into much trouble for fighting in school. Although fighting isn't a good answer, if I had to put up with that bullying for much longer, it's hard to say what would have happened. The curious thing here is that after I stood up for myself, he stopped bullying me; in fact he tried to be my friend after that.

Seems like a strange way to have to earn respect. So, what about the teenager that had taken their life because someone had been bullying them? Did they feel trapped, not sure what to do, or afraid to fight back? I don't think we have all of the answers yet. My daughter was a victim of bullying in high school too. She had to change schools in order to get away from it, and I was pretty upset at how little the school did to stop this. I was lucky though. Things got better for my daughter once she switched schools, and of course I didn't have to deal with this bullying either after my little incident back in high school. But some weren't so lucky.

Referring back to the hospital, something very strange happened just as my dad was taking his last breath. He seemed to be pushing something or someone away. His lips and eyelids had tightened, and he started to use his hand as if he was pushing something away. Whatever it was that he was doing certainly got our attention! He believed strongly in God and Jesus, so I know the Holy Spirit was there to take him home, but to this day I still want to know what that was all about. Could it be someone was trying to pull him away from heaven, could it have been the devil himself?

I just know that it made the top five list as being one of those times when your whole upper body shudders from something you just witnessed, and I wanted to shout out, "What the hell just happened?" After standing there staring at his chest and

SCOTT GESCHWENTNER

wondering if it was going to move again, the doctor was called to the room. We could all tell from the expression on the doctor's face that it was really over. So, I walked out of the room and into the bathroom that was down the hall. I turned on the faucet and let the water run into the sink while I stood there watching it and then I let myself cry. My sisters were still in the room, also bawling, and the poor nurse was just waiting as patiently as she could. My dad was a donor, but because he had cancer, none of his organs were any good anymore, except for his eyes. Of course, they needed to get those out soon before they went bad too. Wow, what an awkward situation to be in. "Can you continue grieving outside the room while we take your father's eyes?" I've heard of parents giving up their child that passed so that their organs can save the life of another child. I can't begin to imagine the pain in doing that. That is a sacrifice beyond belief that I will never understand!

So shortly after my first divorce, I decided to be a volunteer at the children's hospital. This was meant primarily to help keep my sanity coming off a divorce and to keep my mind off of my own problems. I also think I wanted to do it as a way of saying thank you to God for not putting this cross in my life. I rarely had to face the parents, which I think was probably a blessing for me, but while they were at dinner or away at work, I was given the chance to sit with their child and just be. I remember the fun times when I was able to put a little smile on their faces. I can be quite the jokester at times, and I think this quirk of mine came in quite handy during these times, especially since only little kids can really appreciate my jokes. Then there were times when I was asked just to hold a baby and let them scream in my ear in order to give the nurse a little break. My son was a colicky baby, so I had been given a lot of experience. I also was a walking furnace, and those rooms were usually a bit chilly, so once those little babies felt the warmth, they usually had little choice before lulling themselves into dreamland.

But there was one little girl that I will never forget. I had been asked to help with a family whose child was in a very special area of the hospital. And in order to enter this area, I was required to wash my hands for two minutes; then I had to put on a hospital gown, mask, gloves and shoe coverings. The only part of me that was visible were my eyes. The first time I walked into the room, the mother handed me her child as she was heading out for dinner. She kindly asked if I could stay with her child for a couple of hours. Of course when Mom left the room, the child began to scream and her little arms reached for the door where her mother had just walked out. That first hour was the worst, especially when I noticed that only ten minutes had passed. Two hours went by, and I'm not sure who wanted it more for Mom to come walking back through the doorway, but it was a close tie between me and that little girl. By the time the third hour went by, we were figuring "what the heck, we might as well be friends." So, when the mother returned three hours and fifteen minutes later, we were just sitting in a chair sleeping and dreaming the day away. Actually, I was just sitting there from pure exhaustion. The Mom couldn't stop apologizing to me for the extra hour plus some, but I kept assuring her we did okay.

The following week I walked into the volunteer office for my usual coffee and cookies before my shift, and the coordinator walked up to me and asked if I would mind sitting with the

SCOTT GESCHWENTNER

same little girl from the week before. I of course let out an "oh" with about a hundred h's added on, then said sure. But when I walked into the room where the little girl was, at first she started to shy away from me, and then she seemed to recognize me even though the only thing she could see were my eyes. As the mom started to hand her over, her little arms reached out to me. My daughter once said to me that she had never seen me cry, until the day when we had to put our dog down, but those were sad tears. I have to say, the day that little girl reached out to me, I surely couldn't hold back the happy tears in my eyes. But little children seem to have a way of doing that to you. So what is the point to this story? Maybe one doesn't need to look very far to find a reason to live!

So, I thank God that He allowed me to see my dad off that day, having someone taken from your life without any closure is something I don't think we are very well-equipped to handle, at least I know I'm not. I never had the chance to say goodbye to my ex-wife the day she ended her life, but that just shows how suicide is. It's one of those final acts that strips you of this benefit.

Chapter 4

BEING IN THE hospital with my dad that day was one of those moments that will definitely be with me forever. The following day, my mom and sisters were gathered in the back of the church on the day of my dad's funeral, and the casket where my dad lay was open. My mom was talking to him, with us kids standing around, and then she did something a little strange I thought at the time. She was tapping his cheeks saying that it must be driving him crazy that he wasn't clean shaven. My dad, you see, would shave every morning; the guy would even shave if we were up camping. Heck, he would even take the cigarette out of his mouth in order to shave his chin, I mean he was dedicated. I never really understood that. The guys at work used to kid me that I needed to stand closer to my razor.

Anyway, it still seemed very odd at the time, but maybe this was why I had put my hand on her face when I was talking to her in the funeral home that day. I'd been so far away from her while going through the divorce. We were both still living in the same house, which was extremely uncomfortable for me, but there weren't many options at the time. I was sleeping in the guest room, and avoiding her like the plague. She, on the other hand, seemed to be living life as normal and continued with her daily activities as if I didn't exist. Every evening, she would make herself a nice dinner and read a book while eating. After that she would usually lose herself in her garden until night fell. She hadn't said a word to me in months.

When the day came for the service, I showed up at the funeral home a few minutes early, so I was surprised to see that a lot of her work friends were already there. As I walked into the room, I noticed this guy sitting by himself at a table. I had met him a couple days earlier because he worked at the library and I was returning some books I found at the house that she'd forgotten to return. I was a bit taken back because I had not mentioned the service to him, so I was curious how he found out about it and why he was there. She had been spending a lot of time at the library, and to add to my surprise, he even knew where she worked and what she did at work. I wasn't sure why this was happening, but I was trying my best to keep my composure. I asked him just how well he knew her. Then I noticed the ring on his finger, and I asked him if he was married. When he answered yes, I quickly asked why his wife hadn't come. To this day, I don't know the truth, but that was very strange and quite disturbing to me. I do believe this was the beginning of the series of events that occurred over the weeks to follow.

As I said before, Satan waits for the perfect timing, and I don't think I could have been in a more vulnerable state of mind than the one I was in that day. Now more questions were going through my mind, and not the kind of questions I was particularly fond of. More feelings of helplessness, hopelessness and desperation were creeping into my already-damaged world. I suppose God may have had His own timing here, in order for me to deal with this new information. I had begun talking to a counselor about what was happening in my life. Without knowing, I had chosen someone who had similar beliefs, so I had found it easy to open up to her.

As I went through the list of what was happening in my life on the first day, toward the end I told her I was feeling as though Satan had attached himself to my back. It was based on those words that I found out our connection. As we started down this new path, she gave me some words of advice that I hope to never forget. She suggested that when I'm having these disturbing thoughts, I can reject Satan's suggestions by saying these words: 'I denounce you Satan and I send you to the foot of the Cross'. And now whenever I catch myself having these thoughts, I can feel the weight being lifted off my shoulders as I mutter these words.

Satan has no power at the foot of the cross, I remember learning this a long time ago, but I was too young to understand it. You see, by saying these words, you regain your own power and you take away the power given to Satan. I was taught that only God knows your thoughts and motives, so He hears you even when you are praying without vocalizing your needs. Satan however can put thoughts into your head, but he can't read your thoughts; therefore, it's necessary to vocalize when you wish to denounce him. This may sound way out there, especially if spirituality isn't your cup of tea, but I have to say that I was under Satan's attack so many times in those following weeks that I found myself saying these words almost every day. Even so, on-line therapy had continued with her on a weekly basis until she learned of what I saw the day of the suicide. She suggested the use of a trauma therapy that had been used on people who experienced someone's death in their particular role in the military. I suppose the image that I painted of the room that day did not sit right with her either. I must say I really feel for people that have had to go through this type of therapy; it was extremely intense, but I will say it helps the brain deal with what you have seen. And, I'm left to believe it helped because life got easier and Satan was left to wait for my next fall and, boy, did it make me happy to make him wait.

So while enjoying my new found hope, I found myself walking down by the river one day. I wasn't much in the mood to fish, so I knew I wasn't completely back to my normal self, but it felt good to be outside and hearing the river flow past me. For the past several days, I'd been having a very difficult time trying to find a handyman that would repair the room so I could get the house back on the market. And then that's when the thought hit me. I had worked remodeling old homes and doing construction some of the time while going to college. I knew how to do this; the only question was if I could actually walk back into that room and do it myself. So, I decided to check it out, and I left the river and drove over to the hardware store.

Once again, I was having this feeling that I had a shield around me, and nothing could harm me. So having found the supplies I needed, I found myself back over at the house. As I walked in, a sort of calmness remained with me, but there was one bit of uncertainty that had been playing into my doubting mind, so the first thing I did was to make my way into the bathroom. A long time ago I had watched this PBS channel that demonstrated what happens when you flush a toilet. A little off topic here, but what I saw really grossed me out. So, I had this habit where I would always close the lid on the toilet, and even though I had told her about this PBS show, her habit was to always leave it open anyway, and so I had to be sure that the lid was still closed. I know, sad right? but I actually had to do that!

Anyway, once I reassured myself thinking everything was clear, I then walked back into the bedroom, took in a deep breath and started the repairs. The first thing I did was to tackle the subfloor. It actually felt good working with my hands again, it seemed a long time since I'd done that. After repairing the floor and admiring my work, I took out the rest of the carpeting and padding and threw it in the garage. Over the rest of the weekend, I installed a new bedroom door, fixed and installed new window blinds, and filled in a little hole that was put in the wall by something. When I had finished that, I boxed up her clothes and personal items and stuck everything in a storage unit. I was on a mission and I had no idea what was driving me. Before I even knew it, the house was fixed as good as new. I had fresh carpeting installed and then I cleaned every inch of that house. Okay, I know this story caused my daughter to gasp. Heck, I didn't think I would ever set foot in that room again either, but the experience was not of this world. I had been given this suit of armor, and I know that Jesus was walking along with me every step of the way as I entered that house.

SCOTT GESCHWENTNER

At any rate, I was feeling satisfied and somewhat gratified that no one would ever know what happened in that house, unless of course someone told them. This was about the time when the next storm hit. That day she died by suicide; the realtor had come by the house to see if I found out why she hadn't shown up for the signing. Thinking he needed to know, I told him that I found her in the bedroom and that she had shot herself. He already knew that something was up with all of the police presence, and I would have thought he should have known I was in shock. What I didn't expect was for him to tell all to the prospective buyers, I mean talk about filters. I knew the sale would fall through at that point, but I didn't think he would actually tell them that the ex-wife committed suicide by shooting herself in the bedroom. I think it would have been sufficient to say that there was a death, and that the closing would have to be delayed or probably cancelled. So, now my worst nightmare of a suicide in the house was coming true, with much of the thanks going to my realtor.

I think this is what happens when we get in God's way. Now there's a subject where I consider myself an expert. I believe I have gotten in God's way so many times in my life, that He has painted a detour sign on my forehead. The issue with getting in God's way is that He needs to deal with you first so that He can continue His work with the other person that you just got in the way of, and of course, I'm referring to me. Confusing, isn't it? So at one point near the end of the divorce finalization, I decided to just shut up and let go and let God. You've heard that one before, I hope.

Well, I decided to actually take my advice, so I quit bothering her about packing and I stopped trying to get the scoop on what furniture she wanted, or which dishes she wanted to split. None of this had been outlined in our agreement, you know, because she was refusing to say anything. Anyway, so I sat back and handed the reins over to God. It's just incredible how much peace comes along when you can actually do that. I think if I wouldn't have had this peace at the time that I found her in the room, things could have really turned out much worse for me than they did.

So after what happened, the realtor had been apologizing for his little blurting episode, so to speak, and I seriously wanted to end the contract with him after that. I started worrying that if I went with another realtor, then even more people would find out what happened in the house. Before you knew it, this would be all over town and I would be looking at foreclosure and maybe bankruptcy. I couldn't stop thinking of the worst. And I was convincing myself that if I knew what had happened in that house, I sure wouldn't want to buy it. All of these awful words were making their way through my thoughts. Then I started having the discussion with the realtor of what we were going to disclose about the property. From what I was learning, it appeared we were not required to say anything about a suicide in the house. The realtor seemed to have only concerns about his rear end though. I didn't really want to say 'CYA', but that's what I told him. He continued down the path that if someone asked him why the house had been taken off the market that he would be compelled to tell them. This went on for some time and I have to say looking back I wish I had told him to go jump in a lake. But then somehow, we finally both agreed that the only thing that would be said, if asked, was

SCOTT GESCHWENTNER

that someone passed before closing and we had to transfer title. Seemed like a good compromise to me. After all, it was mostly the truth. I just wanted to sell the house and put this behind me, but growing up in the church, I knew only telling a part of the truth was still a lie, so that had not set well with me. But this would have to stay between me and God now, so it played heavily on my mind along with the constant worry I was having of what to say or not to say.

And on that note, I'm back on what the Bible has to say about worry. It is destructive and God plainly tells us just not to do it. Growing up, I always heard the phrase 'be not afraid'. Be not afraid, one of those phrases that are more easily said than done.

Several years ago I decided to participate in this bike ride in Colorado; it was called the triple bypass. This is a ride that starts near Evergreen, Colorado and ends just outside of Vail in a town called Avon. It's referred to as a triple bypass because the ride takes you over three mountain passes. The first is a not-so-well-known pass called Juniper Pass that is located near Echo lake. From there you ride over the Loveland and Vail passes, which might be a little better known. This ride from Evergreen to Avon is a 120-mile ride, which includes these passes that reach an elevation of nearly 12,000 feet. Now, you have to be near insane to do this, because it is a one-day ride, so I had to do it two years in a row. Actually, it is one of the moments in my life that I cherish. But back when I did this ride, there wasn't a bike path from the Baker's exit to Loveland, so we had about a 6 mile stretch of riding on I-70. There's a feeling riding next to an 18 wheel semi-truck that is hard to describe, but I wouldn't recommend experiencing it. When I signed up for this ride, I was terrified. I really enjoyed riding, but somehow sitting on that bike riding 120 miles over three mountain passes was a bit nerve racking. But one day I just decided not to let the worry get a hold of me. I went to the gym every day during my lunch hour and worked the legs. I changed my diet and even quit drinking alcohol, which coming from a father who was an alcoholic wasn't easy, since this hadn't jumped a generation.

So on the day of the ride, I jumped on my bike at 6:00 am and began my 120-mile ride through the Colorado Rockies. All of the determination and dedication I had put into training for this ride really paid off because when I hit Avon a little after 3:00 pm that afternoon, I had such a feeling of accomplishment that I'd never really experienced in my life. If I had let the worrying take over, I may not have ever experienced this feeling which will be with me for the rest of my life.

There's a story I heard a long time ago from one of my teachers in grade school. I don't know the origin of this story, but since I was an avid bike rider, it stuck with me. The story starts out describing life as a bike ride, but this bike is a tandem bike which starts out with me in the front and God behind me helping me pedal. Since I was in front, I had the illusion of being in control. I knew where I wanted to go and what I wanted to see. But somewhere along this road, I decided to switch places with God. It was scary at first letting someone else sit at the controls, I didn't know what to expect, and when I asked a question, God would just smile and tell me to pedal. So when I started to trust that God would take care of me, my life became so much more exciting. He knew how a bike bends in order to take the sharp curves of the road, and He knew what was around the corner before I did, so He was always prepared. I was starting to learn that God was my constant companion and I also had concluded that if I was in control, we would have crashed a long time ago. It is hard for most of us to just take delight in this constant companion we have in our lives, and I don't believe God has ever wanted us to go through life without a physical companion, but there are going to be times in everyone's life when we think we are all alone, and I hope that you're finding out this just isn't true.

So this brings me to the point of this story because another lesson was learned and impressed into my mind once again that day. For from the added stress, and the added anger and frustration, it turned out that the other realtor and the new buyers never even asked why the house had been taken off the market and put back on later. Geez, how much energy had I wasted worrying about this and the grief spent with the realtor? Just goes to show how worrying wasted my already-tired mind on something that didn't even matter in the first place, or in the end for that matter. And then I guess I decided to get back on the bike, ask God once again to forgive me for doubting, and then I began wishing I could just push this stuff out of my mind forever. But maybe this is why suicide seems to be a solution for so many people, a lot of us have this doubting mind and it can be hard to control at times so giving up seems like a simple way just to end it all. It can be a constant struggle for some, but having the ammunition of God's Word is what it takes for me to pull myself out of the abyss I get myself into at times. Maybe I just need to realize this is a dynamic equilibrium, a continuing process to overcome evil. If a TV series became static, what would the next episode be about. Maybe this is why our lives can't become static. Most of us become bored when our lives are static anyway, so we just need to keep plunging forward.

Chapter 5

SATAN SEEMED TO be putting in overtime on me, now he tried to use worrying again in order to try to separate me from God and he was not giving up easily. Once the house had been cleaned up and repaired, and all the signs of the suicide had been removed, the house was ready to be put back onto the market. It was the peak season for selling a house, and I was anxious to get things moving. Of course, there was still this matter of the other party that was on the deed, speaking of my late ex-wife. Now that she was deceased, I was once again back in with yet another legal battle called probate. I had been dealing with the divorce attorney and courts for the better part of five months, so I was not looking forward to dealing with a probate attorney now with even more court time. The divorce had dragged on for so long, and the unknown of the new proceedings was weighing heavily on my already-stressed mind.

The process, however, seemed to start out okay, or so I thought.

The attorney was confident that I would at least be able to keep the proceeds from the sale of the house, seeing that my ex had no children to speak of. She did however have a sister, and I was aware of this, but I had never met or even spoken to her. Something had happened between them; they hadn't had contact in years. My ex-wife never wanted to talk about it, so I decided to let sleeping dogs lie. But keeping the proceeds from the house seemed like the right thing to do. Unfortunately, there seem to be laws out there not concerned with the right thing, and I think a lot of us have come to this knowledge. The divorce decree had given me the ability to list the house and accept an offer, which had been the result of the many motions I had gone through in the divorce. So, when the realtor approached the title company, it seemed we had the green light to proceed. The house hit the market and things started out really well. Within a few hours of listing the house, I had multiple offers. Maybe these events that were happening around me had finally come to an end, or at least slowed down, or maybe it was a result of a really hot real estate market. At any rate, I was only experiencing relief and joy.

We now had a full price signed offer, and it didn't appear that they knew or cared that the house had been removed from the market for a while, so no questions had been asked. We even managed to secure a signed backup offer, which was a first for me. The selling process was moving forward with a strong feeling that nothing could go wrong now, and the time had also been moving along. The next couple weeks had been fairly uneventful and before I knew it, the time had come for the inspection. Even though I was pretty certain the house was in great condition, I was still sitting on pins and needles, as the old saying goes, until I got word that the inspection had gone great and no issues had been found. Yes! I finally caught another break.

Then I get the phone call. I think at this moment Satan had been sitting and watching likely rubbing his hands together in a sinister way, knowing what was around the corner. The title company, in all their wonderful wisdom, notified the realtor that the house could not be sold until probate was complete. This would be months away. Why did they wait until now to tell us that? On top of this news, the underwriter also informed us that they would not accept all of the proceeds going to me, and that they would only insure title if what was outlined in the divorce was followed. This surely wasn't what the probate attorney told me. All of this legal garbage was making its way deep into my life. Now her portion would go into her estate as outlined in the divorce agreement and a judge would decide where the money would eventually end up.

Geez, who makes these laws? Of course, I constantly reminded myself that I was the one who decided the financial split, since she was playing the silent treatment game during the divorce. So, here we are, two weeks prior the title company was telling us that we had the green light, and now just after the inspection took place, we were being told that the entire deal was off. I cannot even begin to tell you the evil thoughts that I was having toward the title company and my realtor. If it weren't for my faith, I dread the thought of what would have happened next. I mean, do you see how Satan arranged these events, or do you think what happened was just bad luck? How susceptible was I anyway? I was just dealing with a divorce that ended in suicide, and a mess that had put me under financial strain. A realtor had let on that he would only be happy if he could rent a billboard on the side of the highway advertising what had happened in the house, and now on top of it all, a title company was killing all hopes and dreams of putting this house and this nightmare behind me.

Once again, I was back in the attorney's office filing more motions and dealing with the courts. If we couldn't find a solution for this, it would take months to complete the probate process. And well, along the way would I have two nickels left to rub together when this was finally over? Then as my hope started dwindling again, a miracle happened in my life. The judge, who had previously denied my application to be the personal representative in her estate, reviewed my situation and reversed his decision. Wow, what a roller coaster ride this had turned into. Initially, he had been wanting the required waiting time to pass, just to see if someone would come out of the woodwork. But then I suppose they decided that I was probably the best option, since I knew the most about her financial affairs. I obviously did not know everything about this person to whom I'd been married for the past six years, but since we had done our taxes together, it would have been pretty hard to hide financial matters from me, or so I thought. Anyway, seeing the dire situation I was in, I think the judge looked at the entire picture and took pity on me and decided to appoint me personal representative. Only by the grace of God! This meant that I could actually trump the title company, at least on the part where they required us to complete probate, and let me tell you, it felt good! I still lost her portion that went to the estate, but at least I could continue with the sale of the house and

SCOTT GESCHWENTNER

put this one behind me. It had become a real nonfiction fight between good and evil, and now good had claimed an edge!

But the fight was far from being over, I think Satan was probably wishing he'd heard about title companies before because they certainly had an evil way of doing business. I believe at this point the devil continued his torment with the title company as his playground. The first couple little hiccups he played on me didn't quite do the trick, but there apparently were a few more that he could try. The next little kink had to do with her estate taxes. I mean really! I realize death and taxes are the two certainties in life, but now we're talking about getting the taxes from a dead person? And let's not forget about the estate bank account. This isn't your typical bank account, oh no, we had to apply for an EIN number to open this account, which treats it as a business. So there seems to be a moral to the story. If you die without a will, and there's money somewhere, now your death is treated like a business and taxes follow you to your afterlife. Whoever said that you can't take it with you? This process had become so time-consuming that at times I just wanted to raise my fists in the air and scream. But maybe this was a good thing now; things were not feeling so personal anymore. Are you sensing any leftover anger here? Yeah, me too, but I'll put this on my to do list for later!

Okay, is this for real? I have to mention, along the way I even tried to switch title companies midstream. My realtor had tried to talk me out of doing it, but I was beyond frustration and really wasn't too concerned with listening to him. Unfortunately, attempting to take this detour just meant more energy spent, and there were only different hurdles snaking their way into an already chaotic situation. Anyway, to continue then, the title company comprised a list of items and sent them over to the probate attorney, insisting that they be addressed before we were allowed to proceed. All along, I'd been trying desperately to hang onto the buyers. I have to express my dismay toward this list of crap from a heartless title company whose only purpose was to add onto the price tag of what I had already spent in the process. But the conspiracy side of me was telling me that this was a way for them to get back at me for the trump card I played on them previously. Obviously, Satan still had a pretty good hold on me. Makes me wonder if I had tried to switch places with God on that bicycle?

In the next couple weeks, I suppose Satan's strategy switched gears since nothing else could be done on the sale of the house at the time. My deceased ex had come over from Europe years before I met her. One of the other things that I had not known about her were the many ties that she had broken off from those she knew over there. Word got out, though, and it truly is still a mystery to me how people clear overseas who hadn't had contact in years found out about her death.

I am not a fan of social media, but to each his own. And, now I feel compelled to give my personal opinion on the subject. It would seem a great way to keep in touch with distant friends and family, and I'm sure a lot of people use it in this way. The issue I have is that it is also a perfect platform for people whom I believe are guided by Satan, to state their false beliefs in hoping others will join them. I read what these people have attempted to do by making up their own religion in order to fit their way of life because the Bible just doesn't fit who they want to be.

SCOTT GESCHWENTNER

Do you really believe God is okay with this? He has given us the Bible, which is His Word, and then someone comes along and suggests not to follow His Word and then hides behind social media to do this? It just seems so dangerous, especially when some of these readers haven't developed the maturity yet to decide for themselves if this is right or wrong.

God has been taken out of schools where we need Him the most because there is always someone that is offended. And some of us ask that if you don't like it, then go somewhere else, but that isn't a solution for them either. Why should they have to leave, they can get their own way right here. I know everyone has their own opinion on the subject, but just look back at the unity that we had as a country when God was put first during the era of the Greatest Generation. I've watched documentaries on the lives these people led, and it is amazing how they stuck together and helped each other. I just don't see much of this in evidence today.

So anyway, getting back to my story, someone overseas attempted to contact everyone over here in the states with my last name to see if they could find someone that would admit that they knew me. Yeah, I know, it didn't seem I had much to worry about but then it turned out that one of them they contacted happened to be my daughter. So, this person overseas claimed to be my deceased ex's goddaughter. Really, I was never told of a goddaughter, and to add to this, my ex had told me she came from a region where just about everyone didn't believe in God, so how could she have a goddaughter? Maybe a goddaughter has nothing to do with God over there? Anyway, it started out as you would expect. She wanted to know how she died, but when we told her, she wouldn't believe us. Then it seemed to turn dark rather quickly. She wanted to know why she had broken off communication with them, and even suggested I had something to do with it. We asked when she had stopped communicating with her, and it turned out that it was years before I had even met my ex. Of course, the accusations didn't stop there, before cutting communication with this person, it was even suggested that I had something to do with my ex-wife's death and that it wasn't even a suicide. Wow, that was so disturbing for me on so many levels that it put me in a depressed state for weeks following. My daughter thought that maybe it was only the way that these people spoke, and she pointed out that this accusation style seemed to be the way my ex communicated much of the time with people. I really was never on the receiving end of this from her, but it has become clear to me now, most people seemed to have felt that way about her. Then again, maybe I was just too close to the situation and just decided to ignore it.

She did have some quirks of her own during the time I had been with her. Being from eastern Europe she had an inescapable accent, and this accent would always prompt the question from someone new asking her where she was from. I finally found out one day why this question had bothered her so much. She apparently just wanted to be a part of something and just fit in instead of always feeling like an outsider. I could understand the part about feeling like an outsider, but wouldn't you have to be ashamed of where you're from to feel this way? I suppose I would need to walk a mile in her shoes. And she also wasn't fond of the way she looked. We once walked into a store where someone came up to her speaking Russian. Of course

SCOTT GESCHWENTNER

she spoke Russian, along with two other languages, but it was very odd listening to their conversation in Russia. Afterwards she was extremely upset that it had happened. She was forced to learn the language when she was young, but she never liked speaking it. And having someone pick her out of a crowd as knowing Russian didn't help matters either. English had been her third language, and although it was my first, I had never really done that well in English class, so communication was difficult at times.

And of course, I attempted to help by trying to solve her problem, which is a normal guy thing. My father's family had come over from Austria while my mother's family had come from some Russian province that had been German-occupied, so I naturally had a very sensitive side to me as a result. I told her that when I was a kid coming into the house after being gone all day, my mom would ask me where I came from and I would always reply that I came from heaven. Don't know where I got that from, but my mom would always answer, "Boy, if you ever get there you better stay there." I guess we could never go for the simple hello. So, when my then wife and I flew to California for a vacation, people would ask her where she was from and she would respond we came from Colorado. And of course, when we took our next trip to Maine where she was again asked the question, she then responded she had come from California but originally from Colorado. Man, I had created a monster. I had been like that all of my life, so I had plenty of practice, but the speed at which she picked that up was quite impressive. My children would always call those dad jokes, but I suppose it could have just been a character flaw. But the other fun thing I'd taught her was to respond in Russian when asked the question. This was actually pretty fun for a while. Whomever was asking the question at the time would turn to me and ask me what she said, but I would of course respond "I don't speak Russian."

SCOTT GESCHWENTNER

Chapter 6

CLOSING DAY HAD finally arrived, and those last few days and hours were the worst. The constant wondering if there was something else around the corner occupied my mind. What else could possibly go wrong? There's that scene in the movie *Jaws* when the captain of the boat is telling the story of when they delivered the bomb, referring to back when he was in the war. I don't know if you've seen this movie, but at the end of his story, he's telling them that after days of being lost at sea, he was most scared during the hours just before it was his turn to climb aboard the rescue boat.

This scene had come to mind when I was thinking of how I'd been feeling that day. So, I had gone in and signed the day before, while the buyers were due to sign the following morning. When I received word the next day that the signing was complete oh what a great feeling that was, now I could really glimpse the light at the end of this tunnel. My realtor told me that I could expect the check from the sale within the hour, so I waited with anticipation. As luck would have it though, this little charade of "what could go wrong will go wrong" continued, and the hour wait I expected turned into five hours. I know five hours shouldn't seem that long, but when the title company is refusing to extend an explanation for the delay, my mind was beginning to fill in the blanks, and I wasn't too thrilled with the blanks. To me, it just seemed to be common decency to let me know what was going on.

So, after hours of waiting, I finally found out that the first issue was with the transfer of the funds, and this had apparently taken nearly three hours to solve. The buyers had taken out a VA loan, so now we had to deal with the bureaucracy that accompanies dealing with the government. Then someone at the title company couldn't fill in the blanks correctly, so the documents were rejected by the county. This didn't happen once or maybe twice. Oh no, this had to go into round three before finally being accepted. I don't know what else went wrong that day that I wasn't told about during this extremely uncomfortable wait, but I was getting unbelievably upset with the title company, and I was letting them know. But, here again, I'm dealing with my old friend anger, and again it was unfortunate for me how I allowed myself to get caught up in the thick of things. But I just couldn't believe this streak of unwanted events would not let up. Of course, this was another one of those times I found myself yelling at God, asking Him: 'Can I be done with this already'? For goodness' sake, can't I just recover from all the crap I've dealt with this year, maybe heal up a little?

But I guess this is what God had decided to do in order to keep my attention. God certainly has a way of dealing with us when we don't want to deal. How many blows did He allow in my life to finally get my attention this year? So of course, it came down to the final minutes before the title company was due to close for the weekend when I finally received the funds, really! It was a good thing that day that the bank was only minutes away, or I would not have gotten the check deposited before the bank closed for the weekend. This had been stressful, not only to put this house behind me, but I was also counting on the funds so my check would clear in order to pay the credit card debt that had been building from all of the cleanup, repairs, and of course all of the aftermath expenses. I really would not wish this on anyone. I'm not even sure how law enforcement dealt with this sort of thing that day. I'm sure this image had been burned into everyone's memory. Even if they deal with this sort of thing more often than I want to imagine, this would seem one of those times that the scene she left would be really hard to forget.

So I would like to give a personal big thank you to the title company. I understand that it was Friday and you were only thinking about the weekend and what you were going to do. Never mind that there were other people involved in this process, I know it is just all about you and everything else comes in second! Oh, that feels good to get off my chest, venting can definitely be a good thing! But I suppose I need to take some of my own advice and practice some forgiving and forgetting. I don't want to admit that I can be lazy on a Friday afternoon too, but hey, no one is waiting on pins and needles for me to finish something before the weekend, except maybe the boss.

Okay, well now I could take that deep breath since the house was finally sold and that nightmare was in the rear-view mirror. At least bankruptcy was off the table. I'd already moved into my townhouse, and I'd already put her stuff into storage, so I could finally get on with my life. With the funeral now behind me, and most of the bills paid off, maybe now I could spend some time healing. But I had to ask "what else have you got for me, Satan, what else can I do for you?" Seems we had been spending too much time together, and it was time for you to get him off my back. So, now that I'd been appointed PR for the estate, I had to make sure everyone had been notified of her death. She had the usual 401k, life insurance and her own bank account from what was split in the divorce, plus some extra I found out about later after being appointed PR, but this would be a story for later. The employer had already been notified of her death; after all, most of them had been at the service. I started to wonder about the 401k and the life insurance. I was also having that uneasy feeling that I was going to be given more disturbing news as time went on, but we know who was helping me with those thoughts, yes!

In the few weeks between the divorce and her death, she had managed to remove me as beneficiary from almost every account she had. I do not know who profited from them, but I do know none of it went to me. Deep down, I knew I hadn't deserved any of that and I would not have felt right about getting it anyway if I had. Except I did feel pretty strongly that the bank account we had split should have been returned to me. Unfortunately, this may be greed talking, but I can attest that most of the money had come from me in the first place. So okay, that was a bit of a blow knowing she went out of her way to make sure the only thing she left me was a mess, but I think I've already said that. Still, I'm pretty sure she was sending me a message. Of course, that was almost nothing compared to what I learned next. You see, I then found out she actually had two 401K accounts one of which I was not aware. The first 401K had been from years earlier when she was married to her first husband, but she actually never removed him from that account as the beneficiary. This I found out by accident, but I'm thinking Satan wanted me to have that little tidbit of information. So, her first ex-husband got a nice little check as a result of her death. Yes, that was another bit of a blow, maybe more of a bit, if I'm honest with myself. Rather peculiar how she didn't change that name after her first divorce. Back when we were married, she had commented to me how she despised him.

Since she was not from this country originally, it seems she really got the shaft in that divorce from her first husband. So maybe it would make sense that she'd just forgotten about the other account. But this knowledge, if true, wasn't really much comfort to me. It was probably a nice comfort for her first ex to receive that money though. And having this new information, I started to wonder if God would have revealed this information to her in death. It wasn't just about the decisions she'd made either, I'd begun to wonder if God had also revealed what I said to her that day talking to her in the funeral home asking for her forgiveness. But what had come to light was feeling very odd to me. Apparently as she was sitting there having already made the decision to end her life, she proceeded to write in her suicide letter where she wanted the rest of her money to go, speaking of the money from the joint account we had split. I can't help but wonder how much hate there was toward me, that even in the last moments of her life she decided to give me that one last jab. Hadn't she condemned me for having an unforgiving spirit?

There is one thought and question that may haunt me for the rest of my days though. I would hope that there was someone else out there who would see the mixed messages that I was getting here? I've already painted this picture that seems to be impressed into my mind, but here she puts on her wedding dress, and I mean she put the flower in her hair, she wore the pearls I bought her, and even put on the wedding sandals, and then to top it off had the wedding videos playing on her laptop. She left me a suicide letter that started out so very heartfelt, but then turned very dark and then returned to being heartfelt, then of course went dark again and this went on for ten pages. I guess this roller coaster feeling was beginning to feel like the norm for me. Oh, and as an added fun note, every law enforcement officer there also got the chance to read it.

But getting back to the other side of the card, she made sure that none of the money was coming back to me. She must have known the mess she would leave behind, she had to have known this would stop the sale of the house. After all, she did this on the day of closing. So was her message that she didn't want the divorce, but since I did that I should suffer and pay for all of the hurt and pain that had been the fault of both of us? Ouch again! Anyhow, suicide can be a selfish act, and as a result, now I was left with the painful knowledge that this act was probably done just to hurt me as much as possible. At this point, the suicide had become so incredibly confusing, and I have to say, my little speech at the funeral home about seeing

SCOTT GESCHWENTNER

her later had started to accumulate a tarnish. I hope this is not true, like I've said before, but she often complained that I had no forgiveness for the lies she told me. I know I tried; I know I asked God to help me get past it. But the un-forgiveness she had for me is also what I prayed for that day as I sat with her in the funeral home. I also prayed that I would forgive and forget this time, so it wouldn't have to follow me for the rest of my life.

And maybe you're still wondering about this other story, the one I so casually alluded to a time or two earlier? Yes, the account she had when we split our joint account hadn't been given away to someone else yet, which had been a bit of luck for me. Turns out, she wasn't able to change the beneficiary, or add one in this case. This bank where she had her funds didn't have any branches in the state we'd been living in, and since they required her to come in person to do this, I guess she figured either to choose not to do it, or just figured it would go somewhere else and I would never know about it. But since I was the personal representative for her estate, I was able to get these funds back from that bank and deposit the money into her estate that I had some control over. Of course, at the time, I didn't think I would ever see this money since we were divorced. And, since she was clear about not wanting anything going to her only sister, this money would probably end up going to the state. Of course, this was not sitting well with me either, but I guess that it wouldn't sit well with anyone in this position. So when the package finally arrived containing the check from her account, I really couldn't believe my eyes when I saw the amount. I had been expecting to see the amount around the neighborhood of what we had split from the joint account, but to my surprise, there was quite a bit more in there. And now here we go again? The person I'd been married to for years had been hiding money from me on top of everything else? I have to say, hadn't I been struck enough blows yet? At this point, I'm feeling as though I just went 15 rounds with a heavyweight boxer. So not knowing what to do, I decided to talk to the divorce attorney about the extra money that had surfaced.

After hearing what I'd found out, the divorce attorney decided to fill me in on some other things that had happened during the divorce. She started out saying to me that none of what she was about to tell me really pertained to the divorce, so she hadn't felt the need to tell me about any of the extra stuff until now. Of course, I dropped into my seat upon hearing this news. I suppose she was feeling I had enough on my plate that I was already dealing with. Apparently, my ex-wife had been calling her saying she didn't want to sell the house because she would end up homeless. She said she had been telling her that she didn't have any money, and she didn't know what she would live on. But the attorney had already known the amount she received from the joint account, and she knew what she was going to receive from the sale of the house, so the attorney wasn't buying into her story. I had been so very confused as to where this money came from that I requested her bank statements, and with the attorney yelling fraud, the bank was forced to comply. So to my worst nightmare, the woman I had been married to had been skimming off of her payroll check and depositing that money into her own account without ever telling me, and this had been going on almost as far back as when we were first married. Wow, what another kick in the shorts that one was. Satan was probably thinking, man, I don't even think I could have come up with this one! And now guess what? I'm back in the divorce and filing a fraud case against my deceased ex-wife. I mean, could it get any stranger than this? And what could be better, now I was back with the divorce attorney, probate was still in process because I hadn't filed her taxes yet, and oh, by the way, now we had this little fraud case that must be completed also before I would be able to close the probate. Then, of course, my divorce attorney drops another bomb on me, since the phone calls had occurred with her and my ex-wife, now she would be ruled a witness. And since a witness can't represent me and be the attorney for me, now I'm finding myself talking to a third lawyer that is handling the fraud case. Believe me, I couldn't make this up. Three different lawyers, court appearances, and judges had become a major part of my life this year, all stemming from a divorce that ended in a suicide.

The year 2020 was pretty hard on a lot of us, and even with all of the crap I'd been dealing with, I knew that there were a lot of folks out there having even tougher times than I was. But I will definitely agree with all of the other unknown friends out there that are very glad to be putting this year in the rear-view mirror. Even with this year behind us, the aftermath of what happened to us may be with us for the remainder of our lives, but it's my dream that the New Year will give us some new hope. For me, there have been many lessons learned, and why God decided to just do it all at once wouldn't have been my choice, but I'm sure He was quite aware of how things were going to turn out. But I suppose this had been His course of action from the beginning in order to get it through my rather thick head.

I hope I will decide to practice what I've learned because I sure don't want to have to repeat this scenario again!

Everything is a process though, at least this is what I believe now, and grieving is one of those emotions that will follow whether we want it or not. But I also feel God has been giving me the tools to help me along. I think about this image of Jesus carrying me through the tough times, but then as I continue forming this image, I start to imagine Jesus offering me some kind words as He slowly sets me back down so I can continue walking on my own two feet. The footprints in the sand start to form light steps until once again there are two sets again. All along the way though, I know He will be there to help me again as I get further down the road.

Back in my early twenties, I found out about this support group that was called Al-Anon. I remember my first few meetings had been a little uncomfortable, since everyone there was talking about their feelings and it appeared, they were there to listen to mine. The one nice thing about these meetings was that you weren't required to say anything if you didn't want to. So, I continued to go to the meetings and sat and listened to the stories about what others went through growing up with an alcoholic. After I'd been going for several weeks, stories began to fill my head, and then one night, there was enough of a long pause between others' stories that someone mumbled a few words. Next thing you knew, everyone was looking at me with great anticipation at what I was about to say, and then it occurred to me that I was the one who mumbled those words. You see, before that night, I think everyone thought I was a mute, so the shock must have been quite something. I know it was for me. And then, I somehow mustered up the courage to tell one of my stories. I had already told the story earlier that my dad wanted me to grow up tough, so I told them the story about when I went to give my dad a hug before I went to bed one night, and as I reached out, he pushed me back and told me I was getting too old for that. I was in the 5th grade. I remember telling the story and thinking it wasn't that big of a deal, and I had started by saying my story is nothing compared to stories I have heard here, but for some reason God had put it in my head to share.

When I finished my story, the look of shock on their faces set me back a bit. Then they began coming up to me and hugging me and giving me words of comfort. It was then I realized that the events that night had probably affected me a little more than I thought. The point of this story is that we all go through stuff in our lives, and sometimes we blow off something that has been traumatic and if we don't deal with it in a healthy way, well, we're just setting ourselves up for more pain down the road. So, I'm hoping you'll learn from my mistake and just do the process! I still find myself sad at times when life gives me a blow, and I can't always jump back from it right away, but at least now I know it is something I need to walk through.

Chapter 7

WELL, THAT LAST one was a rough chapter for me, probably because it had that numeral 6 in the chapter! Yes, some numbers seem to carry a meaning for me, as you will see in the upcoming story. I rarely read the church bulletin, but for one reason or another, I decided to read this one. In any case, I came across an announcement for a course that was being offered which was about resolving conflicts. I'm no longer too proud to admit that I needed this class. God has spent this year making sure of that. So, after some thought, I decided to enroll, and since it was free, how could I lose? There hadn't been a lot of information outlined in the bulletin, so I figured it was a one-night class, but to my surprise, it turned out to be an eight-week course. This information more or less caused me to have second thoughts, I mean how many people can commit to something that lasts eight weeks? Turns out though I had no idea there was so much material on resolving conflict. So, believe me, God wanted me in this class. So I attended the class every Tuesday night for the following eight weeks from 6:30 to 8:30, developing tools to resolve conflict.

Think about it, there's conflict between family members, conflict between spouses, conflicts with people at work, conflicts between parents and children, conflicts between teenagers and on and on this list could go. And I don't think there is anyone out there who hasn't experienced at least a few of these conflicts personally. I realized I had conflicts in just about every aspect of my life, and trust me, it didn't exactly give me a warm fuzzy feeling all over. Not surprisingly, I learned aspects of dealing with conflicts that had never crossed my mind. One of these being that I had moved out of a house where a suicide occurred and into a townhouse with a shared wall where a couple of guys abode whose only goal in life was to drink and party and make a lot of noise. No regard for anyone around them. So, as a result, I went from desiring peace and quiet to demanding it. I was approaching a point in which I was contemplating doing just about anything to get some peace, I mean for Pete's sake I was trying to heal from a suicide.

It's sad how some people can be so incredibly rude, but this is why there is so much conflict and so many wars around the world. Satan spends all of his time making sure these people exist and then others decide to fight back, and of course you know the rest of the story. At any rate, they were stomping on my last nerve, and I discovered that my desire for peace had moved to a very dark place in which I was demanding peace and this was the perfect storm for fueling my anger. This had conflict written all over it, and the part that this class had taught me was that my demand had turned to a form of idol worship. I was beginning to worship an idol which was in the form of peace and quiet. You wouldn't think wanting peace would be a bad thing, but if you think about it, anything good can become an idol when your desire for it turns into a demand.

Forgiveness was another session that proved to be an eye opener for me as well. Over the years I guess I figured that I knew how to forgive, but it would be a cold rainy day in hell before I would forget. I think I'd learned a long time ago that forgiveness means forgiving and forgetting. This is where I'm sure that I was missing it. Yes, my ex-wife deceived me more than once, and I'm sure that I wasn't able to forget because I'd tried to forgive and forget before, but I didn't want to be the fool again because the past had shown me that she would deceive me again. So how am I supposed to do this? Sure, there is this concept that has to do with consequences, which seems to add a grayer area to this already gray concept, but that really didn't add much comfort when you've been on the receiving end of deceit. But knowing the consequences are left up to God somehow leaves me with a calming feeling, even though, this has got to be one of the hardest things for me to do. But I try to remember God promises that if we come to Him asking forgiveness that He will forgive and forget. That is a pretty great feeling to know that God is willing to give us so many second chances, so why can't I do the same? Jesus went to the cross so that our sins would be forgiven. I of course look back and see all of the time I spent on my knees saying I forgive her. But since I was refusing to forget what she had done to me; forgiving might have been in jest. I think it's human nature not to want to look like a fool, so maybe it was the right thing to want to move on without her so I could finally do both of these. Jesus had taught

SCOTT GESCHWENTNER

us not to forgive 7 times but 7 times 70 times. Trust me when I say, I am putting a lot of effort into forgiving now and also doing the other part of trying to forget as well.

The class was going on during the months that I was spending next to these noisy and incredibly rude neighbors, and believe me, I just didn't feel like dealing with any of this. I often found myself going a day without eating again--I had no appetite and I ended up losing more weight during those months. I'm sure I didn't do myself any good allowing the worrying and anxiety to eat me up inside, a concept that you think I would have learned from before. So I was genuinely surprised that I ended up finishing the class. In fact, out of the 20 people that had started the eight-week course, I was the only one sitting there on the last night of class. I don't believe this is pride talking. Like I said, God decided to address this deadly sin in me during the course of an incredibly difficult year. No, I think I wanted to finish the class in order to prove to myself that I had the strength to finish it, and that I still had the power to continue on. God expects us to keep plowing forward despite whatever obstacles get in our way. Somehow this includes making the choice to continue living and depending on God to get us through it.

I wish I could look back and say I trusted God and leaned on Him through it all, but I reached a breaking point. I don't recall ever feeling so depressed. I found myself wondering again if I was in this townhouse situation because I didn't ask God if this was the right thing for me. Maybe there was something better out there for me and I just didn't want to wait for it. Because of my past experience, I'm certain that when I've stopped to ask for God's direction and then actually waited to see which direction I should go, things have always worked out the best for me.

I'm remembering a time when I was considering a decision between two job offers, which was a really nice position to be in. One of the offers was for more money, but I wasn't sure I would enjoy the work. The other job was further away and offered less pay, but it had a better appeal. I remember putting it into God's hands and I'm sure if I would have tried to do it on my own, I would have made the wrong decision. The company offering me more money went into bankruptcy and closed its doors within the year of me taking the other offer. I dread the financial strain I would have experienced if I'd taken that job.

But still, back in real time, I had become so frustrated and so tired that things felt as though I was never going to experience peace and happiness again. The days seemed to drag on, and the nights were even longer. I'm not sure why God allowed me to experience such a dark time again, but I think He wanted to show me that I didn't have the strength to do it without Him; however, with Him, I would be able to get through anything. I often wonder if He planned this little side distraction. Maybe I wasn't ready to really think about the suicide and what she actually did. Sometimes I wonder if this scene in the bedroom were part of a movie, surely most people would sit back in their chairs and say to themselves 'Wow, I really didn't need to see that.' It was quite disturbing.

So one afternoon I spent hours counting my blessings, something my mother always told me to do when I was feeling down

SCOTT GESCHWENTNER

about myself, and I'll bet she never thought I was listening to her. And then I realized my main problem was really just a very noisy neighbor. That is, of course, if we choose to put aside the fact that I was still trying to deal with this suicide thing. Yes, having to deal with them throwing parties every weekend really sucked, and having to listen to their music bang through the wall also seemed absolutely rude. But thinking that some parent would rather fork over the cash just to keep them away from their house gave me a different sense of understanding. I found myself praying for them and then feeling sorry for them, and this resulted in helping me cope a little better with the situation, even though I was still the one left to deal with them.

Although it might be nice just to be a sponge on someone else's bank book, I think in the end I would feel guilty about that. I would continually remind myself that sooner or later, it always catches up to you no matter who you are. Then I began figuring that life was too short anyway, so the townhouse went on the market six months after I bought it. I knew these guys wouldn't leave. Heck, they got to live somewhere on someone else's dime, and I had a lot of living left to do with a hope that this time I'd let God decide where I should go.

I remember getting these words of advice from my dad. He used to tell me, "If you can't stand the 'SOB', pray for him." This has been one of the ways I remember my dad, seems he thought throwing in a curse word or two made his point come across a lot better. In order to do this right, though, you need to exaggerate the curse word. So, dammit, I figured I'd give it a try! Hey, he might have been right about this?

But back to being serious, even the Bible tells us that you should pray for your enemies. Maybe knowing that Jesus tells us to pray for our enemies and He describes doing so as throwing hot ashes onto their head would seem to give most of us an incentive to follow this rule. But it's not what this passage is about. The Bible also talks about how 'vengeance is mine, says the Lord'. So anyway, knowing this, I now try to pray for all of those people with whom I've had the experience of crossing life's path who only care about themselves. These folks have little regard for other people that don't agree with their lifestyle, and I pray something will turn them around. I almost have the feeling that I haven't quite gotten to that forgetting stage again, but I'm working on it now. Maybe being able to recognize it is a good first step for me. And it takes my focus off of someone that is not worth focusing on, and puts my focus back on the people worth focusing on. Wow, that almost sounds like a healthy way to think about it!

With the townhouse back on the market, I found myself feeling as though I was back under the grace of God. The housing market had been booming over the last several months, so at least it appeared I wouldn't be losing money on the deal. And like before, it wasn't very long before I had an offer on the property. But as you would have guessed, God wasn't done with me yet. So, with the townhouse under contract, when my furnace gave out the day before the home inspection, somehow, I wasn't that surprised. And of course, the temperature outside had reached four below zero that night. So when I woke up the next morning, I just knew something was wrong. I threw my hands into the air and figured God was testing me once again in order to see if I had finally learned to trust Him. So I

SCOTT GESCHWENTNER

began calling every HVAC company in the book that morning, and out of the numerous calls I made, only one returned my call. Of course, I only needed one, but before the day was out, I had a working furnace that had been serviced and repaired before the home inspector walked through. And it turned out that I didn't even need any anger to get things done. It's always easier to look back and see the help that you were given, but I think God just wanted to assure me that He was still there. As it turned out, there were a few issues with the furnace, and having these fixed before the inspection saved me a lot of grief.

I would have hoped that God would be happy with how I handled that, but I suppose He needed to top off the tank, so to speak. So as I was sitting at my desk a few days later trying desperately to concentrate on my project at work, I get a short and somewhat incomprehensible text message from my realtor. It read, "The loan is falling apart." What the heck does that mean? I thought to myself staring at the message. You're kidding me, right? Do you think you could have expanded a little with that text message?

With almost no warning, I was weathering the next storm. The person that I was under contract with apparently was failing to qualify for the loan, so it was becoming clear that I would have to start this whole process over with someone else. To make things even worse, the buyer was refusing to give up, even though the bank was telling her there was no way. So now I'm sitting in limbo wondering if I'm going to lose more time waiting for the contract to end so I could find another buyer. This was adding onto my feelings of "why do I need to keep going through this?" Did I feel abandoned, did I feel like I'd been spinning my wheels for weeks and months, was anger creeping back into my life? Yes, looking back I feel that I failed that last test I was given. I told myself, "Guess I just wasn't strong enough."

I have read about people in the Bible, like Job for instance. You read about the trials that God put him through, yet he kept his faith. I'd always hoped that if God put me through the same trials, I would persevere like Job. God brought me close to my limit, and looking back, it was apparent He knew exactly where my breaking point was, but I'd felt defeated. I don't believe that I lost my faith, but I was becoming afraid to talk to God, I just didn't think I could take being told 'no' again.

Now I'm back in the wait state, and this state has become just too familiar to me. Maybe if my head wasn't so incredibly thick, I wouldn't continually be stuck in this state of learning that patience is really a crucial virtue. I guess if I could just accept this... So I was doing whatever I could to try to understand this, but all the reasoning in the world was not really helping much. However, by this time, I was finally figuring out that being angry at my situation wasn't making the waiting go any faster. In fact, it was just making the wait seem longer.

So then here's the funny part of this story, not funny as in ha, but funny as in strange. All along there had been a buyer wanting to secure a backup offer, but my realtor kept persuading me to avoid it, just because it had a contingency that they would have to sell their house first. And since I couldn't see past my own nose, I'm fairly confident I couldn't see God's plan. While desperately trying to lean on God for help one day, I want to

SCOTT GESCHWENTNER

think He set my mind in motion. When the other contract had finally ended, I insisted on going with the backup, and it had turned out to be the cleanest transaction for which anyone could hope. As soon as I signed their offer, they had an offer on their house the very next day. From there everything just fell into place, and the best part is that they offered a little over asking due to their contingent offer, so this little extra covered my other expenses. God just had me wait one more month, you know, because I guess I needed more help with my patience! And once again, I found myself looking back at the events, realizing how they had been engineered for my benefit.

So, once again I was trying to lean on God for help and strength, but there were several weeks during which I just didn't want to pray anymore. I didn't understand why I couldn't catch a break. Please, just give me some time to catch my breath before the next storm in order to give me a chance to recoup and get myself back on solid ground--that's all I wanted. As I stated before, just some time to heal. But I figure this is where God wanted me. If I had been given the time to regain my strength and continue on my own, I might have stopped listening to Him, and I might have tried to jump to the front seat of that bike again. I'm not sure how much more I could have taken, though, but, looking back, I'm positive God knew exactly how far He needed to take me.

Chapter 8

THE SUICIDE LETTER which she left for me started out by saying the day I asked her to marry me was the happiest day of her life. I should have stopped there, but then I read the next sentence. How or why the letter changed so drastically to then telling me that I had no forgiveness and that I had never trusted her from the beginning was quite upsetting and a little hard to read, especially given the state of mind I was in at the time. We had tried couples counseling a few years previous, but that turned out to be a disaster. I had hoped that someone else explaining how a person feels when they've been deceived would somehow give her a better insight to my concerns. She, on the other hand, had a different idea of what she wanted from the counseling, but this probably isn't all that unusual once a relationship has reached that stage. To make things worse, I also believe I'd chosen the wrong person for the counseling job. I firmly believe the right person could have steered the session so our dual frustrations would have been addressed and maybe even solved. But of course, I've got to go back to the beginning where I'm left to conclude that maybe God did not want this union, and maybe it wasn't in His will to have the relationship fixed? I can only assume this because of the time I spent on my knees asking God to help me move forward from this dark place I was in. If it was His will, I don't think I would be sitting here writing about what transpired over the past year. But this leads me to the question of how then do I listen to God? I have tried to spend time in God's Word just about every day by reading my daily devotion and asking God for His guidance.

One of the reasons that I love to fly fish is because I can usually find a quiet place where I'm not distracted by outside influences. There is a refreshing calmness that I always experience when I'm standing in the middle of the river feeling the rushing water go by. The pressure of the water against my legs, the sound of the river that drowns out the noises of the world around me, and the warm sun on my back puts me in a place where I can just stop and listen. And then every once in a while, there's the train that comes roaring by along the side of the river. There's always a moment of sadness when the train has passed by, but then the sound of the river returns and I'm back in my place of listening again. It's a piece of heaven to experience, and somehow being so close to heaven, I believe I'll hear the voice of God.

The life we each lead has always been a journey, and this turns into a journey through grief when an event such as suicide happens in our lives. The all-important factor is how we process the events in our lives. I was blessed with having family that helped me walk through this grief, but whether you have lots of family and friends or you're by yourself, Jesus is always there to help carry you through it. This is the main reason I wanted to include the poem at the beginning. I will probably carry a little bit of sadness around for the remainder of my life, but that's okay, I just need to continue my journey. It has been really fun writing and sharing my experiences, but along the way I also realized how I have lost some of the pieces of my life that I had when I was younger. Everyone probably has had this happen to them for whatever reason, but I miss some of the old me sometimes. Maybe I've already experienced Heaven. I've looked into the eyes of my young children as they smiled back at me, I watched them as the training wheels came off of their bikes and witnessed their joy. I saw the freedom they experienced when they took their first ride alone in their car, and a thousand other little things along the way. It has been a wonderful journey.

One day my daughter asked if I believed in reincarnation. Not really, I said. I think this comes from an eastern religion. I don't believe there is anything in the Bible that supports it. But sometimes it's just a little fun to think about. I've often wondered about God's sense of humor. Just look around at what He has created and you have to wonder: was God having a good time that day?

I've also had the thought that if a person is extremely hateful toward another race, after you die, would God send you back as a member of that other race? Wow, that might just fix a lot of problems if we all believed that one. So, then my daughter told me about this red bug that had been following her around everywhere, and the thought crossed her mind regarding whether

SCOTT GESCHWENTNER

it could be my ex ; after all, the timing was right. Where she made that connection, I'm not entirely sure. That kind of sounds like a great children's story book though.

But this brings up another mystery of suicide. In the 10 Commandments we find: Thou shall not murder, and suicide falls right under that heading. Suicide is murdering yourself, isn't it? This is why it is so alarming for us or at least so alarming for me. This is a very violent act against oneself. No one knows how God really deals with this, in my opinion anyway. The Christian church has had many different views dating back to nearly its beginning. Suicide was regarded as a sin in the church I grew up in, and we were taught to think that if you killed yourself that you were doomed to hell. Catholic doctrine wasn't even settled on the subject until the 17th century when they changed their viewpoint taking into account the state of mind the person must be in in order to do this to oneself. It appears there have been many different views on the subject, and although I've expressed my views here, attitudes vary greatly depending on many factors. My point is that everyone can't be right. God forgives all sins, well except speaking sacrilegiously and rejecting the Holy Spirit's presence in your life. That sin will not be forgiven according to the Bible. But if the sin is confessed to God and you really have no intention of repeating it, then God forgives. Let's just say we accept this. After all, I think most of us do. The commandment states thou shall not kill, which includes yourself. So, if you die by suicide, when could you possibly confess your sin to God? While standing at the gates of heaven waiting to be judged? It's a bit of a scary thought for me--this unknown.

But to continue picturing life as a journey, there have been some wonderful stories along the way too. Once I got through college, I decided that I needed to start enjoying life more. For the previous seven years, my life had consisted of work and school--there wasn't time to do much of anything else. So with college in the rear-view mirror, when Friday night finally rolled around, my Jeep buddy and I would flip a coin in order to figure out which direction we were going. Heads meant west and tails meant north. As we headed to the hills, so did our worries. We didn't care where we slept, we had a tent and a couple sleeping bags and didn't need very much of anything else. I may have been a little too carefree one weekend when I opened up the tent in the morning and found myself staring at a bunch of cows. Seems the night before, we'd pitched the tent in somebody's pasture. I have to say, the cows looked just as confused as I was.

This memory brings back some good feelings for me, and although I may have been a little too carefree, I still wish I had some of that me back. Tragically, when we were making our way back down the winding road the next day, we followed a motorcycle that was racing too fast around the winding curves of the road. As we made our way around one of those sharp curves, we saw the motorcycle off in the trees and the two passengers lay near the side of the road. The guy did not survive the crash, and the girl wasn't in much better shape. Since this was in the days before cell phones, my buddy had to drive down the road to get help, while I stayed with the injured woman. I placed my sleeping bag over her to keep her warm, and then sat with her, continually asking her not to move.

When the ambulance finally arrived, they took the guy and then called the flight for life for the woman. I remember her telling them that she didn't want to go because she didn't have insurance. Quite the sad state of affairs. She'd lost her friend that day and, although I never found out her outcome, I suspect she never walked again.

And back in those younger wilder days, we used to cliff jump. As old as I am now, we might have been the ones who discovered it. Anyway, we had a favorite spot on the river where we'd jumped off more times than I can remember. One day we heard on the news that someone else had jumped off from that same spot but hit a rock as he landed. This turned him into a quadriplegic overnight. We'd swam around that area and checked for rocks, maybe he was just a few feet off, one way or the other, but either way my jumping days had come to an end.

Seeing the motorcycle crash had also made me more cautious. I know one thing for sure, my Holy Spirit had been working overtime in order to protect me, so it finally occurred to me one day that He must want to keep me around for some reason, and for that I am grateful. Though looking back, I sometimes wonder if we really grow out of it. When I was given the chance to take my kids to Disneyland one year, one of our goals was to ride the roller coasters, well, at least it was one of my goals. Maybe this is just clean fun, but there's a reason we ride them--they scare us to death. Maybe there isn't a real threat, but accidents have happened. Besides, I went to school with guys of this generation who designed these rides, and that there is scary enough for me!

One day back in college, my roommate got a phone call from his parents. His younger brother had been riding a 4-wheeler the night before and had gotten into an accident. Unfortunately, he died from his injuries that morning. My roommate and I had known each other for a couple years at this point, so we'd become fairly close. He knew I was spiritual and I knew he could take it or leave it, but we respected each other's viewpoint anyway. And while trying to comfort him the day he received this horrible news, which was very hard since I had not dealt with this kind of thing before, he turned to me and, with a very serious look on his face, asked me if I thought his brother had gone to heaven. Boy, talk about putting someone on the spot. Although we had known each other's position on God, we had never really spoken about it with each other. I'd known his family wasn't religious, in fact I remember having a discussion with his mom in their kitchen one day. She was very thoughtful about my beliefs; I think she was just very curious because she'd never been exposed to God much growing up and I thought that was sort of sad. So anyway, I asked him what he thought, but he just sat there shaking his head not knowing what to say.

It's odd how death often brings up the subject of God, when no one wants to talk about Him any other time. I don't recall exactly what I said at the time, but I remember telling him that God is all good, and even if his brother didn't know who Jesus was while he was still alive on earth, God was going to give him another chance in heaven. And then I told him that his brother was a very smart guy, and I'm sure he gave God the right answer. Well, at least we ended up laughing at that for a while, then we spent the rest of the day talking about all the fun and crazy stuff he did with his brother growing up.

SCOTT GESCHWENTNER

But this story is part of the reason that I'm writing this book in the first place, I'm hoping for more of us to get to know and accept Jesus before it is too late. I jokingly told my roommate that his brother would be given another chance, but this is true and this is also stated in the Bible. I'm sure there are a lot of people around the world that have never even been given the chance to know God, but this is part of the reason we are sent out to spread the good word. Even with this second chance, for me, if I had not known who Jesus was, it would seem difficult just to accept something that I had not been previously exposed to.

And it is sad that his story didn't end there. I moved back to Colorado, but I stayed in touch with my old roommate. One day he called to tell me that his mom had lost her battle with cancer. That was hard enough to hear, but then he told me his little sister hadn't taken her death too well, so she went into the garage, closed all the doors and started the car. I didn't even know what to say. I wasn't even able to comprehend all of the death he'd had to deal with. His sister was one of the most caring and loving spirits I ever met, and I just couldn't understand that either. Suicide has a way of tearing pieces out of everyone involved, and I am still deeply saddened to this day that she died that way.

And I'm finding that suicide doesn't discriminate because of your age either. Coming out of college, I landed a job working in a research division that was part of a university. This was quite a few years ago, but working at a university had some nice perks back then. I'd been there going on a few years when I was asked if I would consider working in a different division for a while. They were in need of electrical help. So, I jumped over into the physics division for a while. After I'd been there three or four months, I was coming into work one morning and as I passed the front office, I noticed quite a few people standing around. The scene looked a little dismal. Some of the women had tissues against their noses, others were standing around with their fingers pressed to their eyes.

Well, I just kept walking to my office, and when I sat down the guy in the next office to me informed me of the situation. One of the scientists, and I would have to guess that he was in his seventies, had put a gun to his head the previous night. Okay, that was a bit of a shock. I had spoken with this guy a few times, as he was always bringing me equipment that he wanted calibrated or repaired. I always thought that, for a scientist, he was sure down to earth. When he'd come into my office, he'd kind of lean over and whisper 'I know this isn't in your job description, but would you fix this thing for me?' Actually, it was my job description. I think he just liked acting like a character. I never knew if he'd been married or if he had kids, so it's a mystery to me why he did this. Maybe it's just human nature that wants the answer to this question, why?

And, as I'm writing about these friends I've known, unfortunately, more have come to mind, which causes me to think that there have been a lot of people affected by this senseless act. And after doing a quick search on the web, it appears that this is well within the top 10 causes of death worldwide. I hadn't realized up until now how many people I have known that chose this fate for themselves. Even looking back to when I had my own small business, I was doing some work for a customer

SCOTT GESCHWENTNER

in Kansas. I'd been out to see him several times, and I knew he had a wife and a small child. Looking in from the outside, I would have guessed this guy had it all. But one day I got word he had placed his shotgun into a wood vise and then used both barrels on himself. This was the sort of news that just forces you back against your chair asking 'is this for real'?

Years ago when I was in the Boy Scouts, in the summer between the seventh and eighth grade and I attended the week-long Jubilee Boy Scout camp. It was a chance to earn a few merit badges in a week's time. I think for most kids, this was a time to get away and have some fun.

Being a late bloomer or slow learner, whichever label you wish to use, this summer camp was a pretty stressful time for me. The year before, I'd come back with only one merit badge, instead of the three I went for. Well, I'll never forget the disappointment my dad blasted me with, so the following year I was determined to earn all three, and I was prepared to die trying. One of the badges that I was going for that year was called the wilderness merit badge. What I didn't know at the time I signed up for it was that we were required to sleep out in the forest all by ourselves for one night during that week. Now, I'm not sure how the other kids felt about this, but just coming out of the seventh grade, I could have wet myself. When the day came, the scout leader marched us out into the wilderness. Of the five boys that decided to do this ludicrous exercise, there was only one other kid from my scout pack. As we headed out about noon, we arrived at the first site when the leader pointed at me and said 'you will be staying here'. They had let us bring our canteen, a few matches and a knife, but we weren't allowed a sleeping bag or anything else for that matter, and being the first one dropped off, I had no idea where the other kids were.

Anyway, the day started out okay. I was given six or seven hours to build some kind of fort before night fell on me; and things weren't too bad in the light of day.

Now, I wasn't an experienced contractor and the art of log house building hadn't been a prerequisite, but I knew it couldn't be done in six hours. So, I created a makeshift fort with the branches and logs that I could move by myself. After a few hours of working on my shelter, I took a step back and figured it was good enough for one night. Of course, thinking back, I'm sure a little girl from the fourth grade could have done a better job, but anyway, it had become time to start my camp-fire. As I'm sitting here writing about this, how silly was it to give a seventh grader some matches and tell him to go build a fire in the woods? Okay, anyways back to the story. Now night was falling, and I'd taken out the candy bars that I'd secretly stuffed into my socks before heading out. My fort was pretty close to the fire, but since it was also made out of wood, prob-ably wasn't the best choice, but again I wasn't the sharpest tool in the shed. While sitting next to the fire, the darkness of the night snuck up on me rather quickly, and my eyes were held open to nearly the size of my head. I think fortunately since I'd known about this night for the past two days, I hadn't slept very well, so my body shut done without getting much of an argument from me.

Sometime during the night though, the kid from my scout pack had found his way back to my site. I think I had been in

SCOTT GESCHWENTNER

a pretty deep sleep when I heard sticks breaking from someone walking toward me. Luckily, he called out before getting too close, because I had clinched the knife in my shaking hand, not really knowing what I was going to do with it. I could see that he was just as terrified as I was, so we sat up most of the night talking. He had been trying to persuade me to go over to his camp, but I was having nothing to do with moving for fear I would lose the merit badge. Then sometime during the night we both fell asleep, so when we were awakened by the scout leader the next morning, I could see the relief in his eyes when he found out the missing kid had found my camp during the night. We both survived that night and we both received that merit badge. So a few years later, when I learned he'd put a gun to his head, I thought back to this story, remembering how we'd been there for each other that long and rather scary night.

And I wish it could have ended long before this last one but there was a classmate in high school who was yet another victim of this horrible act. He was an extremely bright guy, even earning the valedictorian. I believe he sought his fortune working in commercial real estate after college. I'm not sure what happened, but somehow, he found himself in bankruptcy. I remember the pressure he had put on himself to be the best in high school, and I would have to assume he was feeling as though he'd completely failed in life just because of some financial deal that went bad. I know this type of pride was coursing through my veins at one point, so in a way I can understand it, but at the same time, I would never be able to relate to this act of violence toward oneself.

My roommate's little sister had taken her life the day after her mom passed, and from what I remember, it had only been days after discovering he was bankrupt that my high school class-mate also took his life.

The scientist appeared to be a statistic, being over 70 years of age. Maybe a guess would be that he felt he was a burden to someone, but how sad it would be to be labeled a statistic? I would say that you had a brilliant mind and I am sorry that you felt you had to leave us this way. For my business customer that I mentioned, nobody even knew anything was wrong. I actually remember looking forward to seeing him as he had this contagious laugh that just made you feel good to be around him, but was his laughter covering up some dark side that he was dealing with? Would this be another label of some type of mental disorder?

I was curious to find out the why for my ex-wife's act. I wanted to know where and when she'd bought the gun because I wasn't even aware that she had one. I'd called the detective a month or two after the incident and asked the question. When he re-turned my call, it seemed apparent to me that he understood why I'd been asking for this information. Although he wasn't allowed to tell me where she bought it, he told me she bought it about five weeks before the day she took her life. Five weeks worked out to be within a day or two of when the divorce became final, so it seems she had planned this thing for that same amount of time. They say suicide is often impulsive, like it probably was for my roommate's sister. There are, of course, exceptions, but knowing that she had this gun for five weeks but used it on herself the day of closing leaves me to assume much more was going on here. This act against herself wasn't

SCOTT GESCHWENTNER

just about her. It seems clear she was definitely sending me a message as well. Maybe this one was just too close to me, and maybe it isn't fair to be comparing the situations and reasons for why these others ended their lives, but the day she pulled that trigger we both lost.

I've read about the five stages of grief in several books, and as I sit here and vent with ink, the thought occurs to me that she may have been stuck in the second stage of anger on top of everything else that was going through her mind. And, as I've pointed out before, this is one topic I've had experience with. The first stage of this grief process is denial, and this would seem to coincide with what was happening during the divorce, but what is so difficult is the complication of putting two lives together when each are at different stages in this process. As if suicide wasn't hard enough, now I'm finding myself dealing with the stages of grief not only from the divorce, but also her death, and I can't help but feel I'm in a different stage of the grief process from both. I wonder if there are some psych professionals out there saying 'you might have something there!' Well, not sure I really figured anything out, but one thing's for sure: there has been a lot of energy spent thinking about it. Okay, so she probably was angry. So now what? Does the question change direction as to why she was stuck there and not able to get into the next stage? And why did suicide seem her only answer?

Chapter 9

GETTING BACK TO the statement I made earlier about the number six. This number seems to have a significant meaning to me, and as you will see, numbers are one of my little quirks. The number seven has a good meaning in the Bible. One doesn't have to get very far into the first book of the Bible before reading that God created the world in six days and then He rested on the seventh. Who really knows how long a day was back then? I want to think this may have been God's way of relating to us, since we are bound by time.

The Bible is arranged in seven divisions--three are in the Old Testament and four are in the New Testament. In case you are unaware of these divisions, the chart is laid out starting with the Law, and then the Prophets, along with the Writings complete the Old Testament. The New Testament starts with the Gospels, and then the General Epistles, Paul's Epistles and finally the Prophecy make up the other four. I would encourage you to have a good understanding of the New Testament before reading this final book, Revelation. The prophecy may put the fear of God into you. I'm not sure how many times I have read this book, but I still don't feel as though I understand it. And I really don't care for the number six;

I think some people feel the same about thirteen. My dad was buried in section thirteen of a military cemetery. I sometimes try to add cosmic significance to numbers; this is my own twisted mind at work, so I wouldn't read too much into it. Speaking of 13 though, that is the sum of six and seven, two numbers that have significant meaning in the Bible. And how about Jesus and the twelve disciples? That gives us a total of thirteen too. What does this actually mean then? Probably nothing, it's just a fun exercise my brain enjoys. So I'm not entirely sure if the number thirteen is a good or a bad thing. Maybe that only applies to the stories in a building or a Friday of the month.

But I once passed on making an offer on a house just because the street address had two sixes in it. I mean one more six and we're talking about the sign of the devil, right? Probably just a "me thing"! But there are even other references to the numbers six and seven. God had Joshua march around the walls of Jericho for seven days, the first six days they marched around the wall six times and on the seventh day they were told to march around seven times. When they did this, the walls of Jericho fell down and they began entering into their Promised Land that God promised them. This seemed like a logical thing to do, yes? Maybe when we're looking for answers from God, we shouldn't dismiss the things that seem strange to us. "That'll never work, what are you, crazy?" Think about it, so many stories in the Bible just don't appear to have logic, and by that, I mean human logic.

Next time God tells you to walk around in a little circle and talk to yourself, just do it! Anyway, if you are not familiar with the sixes and the devil, you will understand this reference once you have read the book of Revelation. I don't want to paint the wrong picture for you of this book, but I would strongly suggest that you be with someone that understands the writings. Society and Hollywood have distorted words like Apocalypse or Armageddon used in this book to leave you with the impression that the end of the world will be a nightmare like you have never experienced. The truth is that it will be for people that haven't accepted Jesus as their savior. If you have put your trust in Jesus, this is good news, but again, don't take my word for it. I hope this will encourage you to read and understand the New Testament.

And, even though the Old Testament was written thousands of years ago, it is quite amazing how it applies today. Early in my career, I had the pleasure of working with a guy who was very open to discussing the Bible. The only problem I had with this was that he liked to take passages out of context and turn them around into something bad. I should have started by saying I had the unpleasantness of working with him. I usually wasn't very open discussing spiritual matters. I was always of the opinion this was a personal matter for most. Somehow though, he determined I was a religious guy, so he had zoned in on me. This might have been a blessing for me, though, because it forced me to re-read the Bible in order that I could rebut his

SCOTT GESCHWENTNER

biblical notions. You probably remember my views about social media; who could forget that one? And I'm sure you have either heard or read the eye for an eye and a tooth for a tooth passage that some use to justify their own evil, as my previous co-worker did. The passage, if taken literally, has this meaning for some; but could this actually mean let the punishment fit the crime? Jesus addresses this passage in the New Testament, and it may seem that Jesus is revoking the passage, but instead He is giving the responsibility to the correct authority. It's our responsibility to love our neighbors and enemies. Satan knows every word in the Bible, you can bet on that. This is one of his weapons for turning us toward him. He uses the Bible, turning and twisting the passages around so you will allow evil into your life, and he is a master at doing this.

So, life goes on. The sun still rises every day and I still get out of bed and try to make the best out of the day, at least most days anyway. And again I know that there's a reason for what has happened this past year, God allowed this to happen, and I can accept that He allowed it to happen; but as I said before, I'm not sure I'll ever really know why.

I once wrote a letter to my kids and some of what I wrote went like this: "We can always choose how we process the events that happen in our lives. We can be happy despite our circumstances, even if a fiercely challenging obstacle such as a suicide is put in our way. Happiness has never come naturally for me. Maybe this is true for most of us, but we shouldn't expect to work past this in order to arrive at happiness. Happiness is in the process, and that seems for me to be a healthy way to process the events in our lives. Life will be challenging at times, that's the planet we're on and I believe God designed it that way. It is part of the growing process, yes? Jesus knew defeat, the Agony in the Garden, but He accepted this only for our benefit. It is all about who we become in the process anyway. God has given us all the tools to overcome every roadblock that has occurred in our lives, which is why He blessed us with the Holy Spirit the moment that we accepted Jesus as our Savior. Just enjoy your journey; I know I am trying every day to get back to enjoying life so I can once again enjoy my journey."

Everyone in life will most likely have to deal with the death of someone they love in their journey. I was very sad the day my dad passed, but I also knew he was in pain and his quality of life had approached zero. My former wife had a difficult life, and like most of us, made some pretty bad decisions along the way. I know for a while that we'd been happy together, but something was tearing us apart and I couldn't seem to fix it. Knowing that I may never see her again is a difficult thought, and I know once I have completely forgiven her for what she left for me, it may become an even more difficult thought to process. But I also know God will show me what I need to know, so maybe I can finally turn the reins over and just enjoy the ride. I'm hoping that I will make it to heaven someday, and I'm hoping to see my dad again one day. I know he was pretty rough on me growing up, but being a dad myself has given me a better understanding. I also hope to see my dog too. They say all dogs go to heaven, so I hope to find out this is true. When my dog, Springer, died, I was still married, and I remember how she cried with me. She said she was going to miss his greeting at the door the most. You see, when we were first married, she worked the night shift, so most of our time together was spent on the weekends. I would usually be gone for work in the morning before she returned home from work, but Springer was always there to meet her at the door.

I'm confident that Satan is waiting and watching for the next event to come along so he can once again become closely involved in my life. I realize God knew what the outcome of these series of events would be which started when I filed for divorce. I know He wanted to make me a more patient person. He may have initiated the times that I was forced just to wait. Patience is definitely a virtue. He also wanted me to work on my anger. Anger often involves an unforgiving spirit, and the compassion that flowed through me when this happened gives me some hope that I can integrate this too. One of my favorite passages from the Bible is from Romans, "Affliction produces endurance, endurance produces proven character and proven character produces hope." I'm sad that He allowed her to go through with the suicide, but I like to think God figured she had experienced enough pain in her life and it was time to bring her home. And God has given us free will, and this free will could also be the reason God allowed this to happen. I do hope one day God will enlighten me and answer most of the why questions in my life, but I'm also thinking maybe these questions won't matter so much in heaven.

Looking back at myself, I am sure glad that I got out of God's way. God has a plan for each of us. I do believe that statement, but I don't want to ever assume that I know what God is thinking. I still have a lot of questions, but I'm learning a little every day about the fact that I need to start letting go. I don't know why some people have seen so much pain, while others seem to coast through life unaffected by anything. But God has promised all of us a perfect, wonderful life in heaven which has been given to us because we believe in Jesus. However, we are required to face and accept the trials and tribulations that happen in this life before we can get there. For myself, I'm going to keep running the race and when times get tough again, I'm just going to keep my eyes on heaven!

As I write this final chapter, I'm realizing that things have calmed down. But since I'm still a glass half empty sort of person, I can't help but wonder what's around the next corner. I've pasted a note on the front of my computer that says 'Ask God.' I hope this message gets sunk into my head so the next time I want to make a life-changing decision that is not good for me, I'll hear God telling me "no." I should capitalize that and underline it and then even change the font to something that really stands out! I've also decided that I want to surrender my life over to God, I desire the life portrayed in the story of the tandem bicycle–putting God in charge. I've had a good life, but I've made enough mistakes trying to do things on my own; so I thank God for helping me along the way, even when I didn't ask for help, but obviously needed it. This is my way of giving God His glory for all the times He has been there for me in my working, playing or even my resting times. "Praying about everything," "fighting your battles on your knees" are phrases that I've been learning and trying to follow.

Unlike my 3rd grade experience. Yes, you'll have to bear with me one last time, I have to go back in time a little and finish the story I started several chapters ago. Go back to a time when my third-grade teacher wished she had never become a third-grade teacher. It was the only year that I didn't miss one day of school, and I remember even getting a certificate at the end of the school year that said 'no days missed.' That's the year my teacher probably wished I would have been absent at least once in a while, and I can only assume this because I noticed the groaning and shaking of her head when she handed me that certificate. Yes, I'm not sure what this story has to do with this book, but I think it has to do with the people that God put into my life. Years ago I learned this teacher had passed on at a pretty young age. I think it was some kind of cancer, and hopefully not my antics, which finally took her home to heaven. Sometimes I feel God takes the really good ones too early. Maybe they just were not meant for this earth. Anyway, I want to say thanks to my teacher and also to say sorry for all of the chalk I used while writing on the blackboard "I will not fight in school, I will not fight in school..."

So getting back to the present, I certainly will never forget this year, and I'm so grateful that I didn't know what was in store for me when the year started. I have caught myself looking back and remembering the lonely times when I was definitely stuck, but I am not allowing myself to think about it and remain stuck on the thought anymore. My new weapon for handling these bad memories is to mentally grab the bad thoughts and physically throw them out of my head, in a mental kind of way. This really works great for me, and maybe it will work for you as well! I have really enjoyed revisiting my past, and this writing has helped me to cope and understand a little bit better regarding the events of this past year. During the course of the year, my work project unfortunately came to an end as well, and now I am looking for my next adventure. I have been laid

Happy Healthy @ peace !

off from a position before, but with everything God has been
teaching me during this past year, this time I am not afraid. At
the very least, now I have the time I need to heal. One other
thing I know for sure, even though Satan may be watching and
waiting around the next corner for me, I know God will be
there too. I'm not sure how I will feel tomorrow, but today I
(am happy, healthy, at peace and it feels great!)

It may be hard to believe, but I have some good memories
of this day as well. The day that I found her in the room, I
called my boss and my mom and even the lady working on
the financing for the townhouse with whom I'd been under
contract. I've already told the story of the phone call I had with
my boss, and someday I may want to apologize for that, but
it seems very odd that the lady doing my financing was a rock
for me that day. I wasn't thinking very clearly at all, and maybe
that is obvious as to why, but she was actually giving me words
of advice that really helped in keeping me grounded that day.
The thoughts I was having about the suicide and the house and
where I was going or what I should do was all put into perspec-
tive by her words. It was truly amazing. I'm positive God put
this person in my life just for that reason.

My mom was floored when I called and told her the news, but
she managed to tell me that I needed to make sure and take
care of myself. This was some devastating news to everyone,
but my mom knew how important it was that I continued to
take care of myself so that I would be able to deal with the situation. The other call I made was to my daughter. I had been
very hesitant in making this call, because my daughter was still
recovering from having her tonsils removed. This procedure is

not much of a big deal if you're a child, but she was a young adult, so this sort of procedure was considerable, to say the least. I had had my tonsils out as a kid, but the only thing I remember was all the ice cream I ate. There wasn't anything wrong with my tonsils, but my two older sisters were having issues, so the family doctor convinced my parents to have my tonsils taken out at the same time, kind of a three for two deal. I don't remember having much to say about it at the time. I just recall being told that I would be able to eat all the ice cream that I could ever want. So, when I didn't get all the ice cream I ever wanted, like I was told, I got out of the hospital bed and took the ice cream from my sisters! We were all in the same room, so it was fairly convenient to take theirs. Of course, the nurse felt differently about it, but I really didn't like her very much anyway. I remembered that shot in the butt she gave me when I woke up tonsil-less!

So anyway, I finally decided to call my daughter and tell her the news. I suppose it was the shock of what happened, but she started to cry and the last thing I wanted was for her throat to start bleeding from crying. Her voice had changed to a high pitch because of the surgery, so you just couldn't help but feel sorry for what she was going through. The last thing I wanted to do was add onto the stress of an already stressful situation. It was still good to hear her voice; she had gone back to Colorado to have the procedure done where her mother was, so I was alone in the state of Montana dealing with the suicide. I really didn't want to be there; I remember having such a desire to jump in the car and just start driving. But talking to my daughter helped calm me down. Of course I was continually being interrupted by the events going on that day, so when my son called me, my daughter had already given him the news. It was odd to hear him reassure me with the words: "You know, it had nothing to do with you."

I realized that day how much God had blessed me. I don't know why He gave me such great blessings, but I just want to be thankful and not ask for reasons why. Having my kids there for me was a godsend. So when I asked my daughter if she would proofread this book, she responded, "Sure Dad, it's not like I haven't heard these stories a hundred times before!"

I'm pretty sure she gets her sarcasm from her brother? But in all seriousness, I now live with the fact that my once-wife made the decision to take her life and this decision was her own. But I also know that it didn't help matters that I rejected her. I still believe this doesn't give anyone the right to take their life, but if you are in the state of mind that says there is nothing left for you, I'm sure what I did didn't help matters. Still, I'm trying not to put any extra blame on myself for what she did to herself; but like I said before, I am extremely sad for her, and I wish she would have chosen life. However, I guess I can now finally rest in the thought that for her there will be no more crying.

Hopefully, reading about my journey has comforted you in some way and, hopefully, made you a bit wiser and humbler. If you have made it this far, maybe some things have come to light for you. I know that my thoughts have become clearer to me by writing about what transformed over the past year. All along I've been trying to put more faith in God, and although it has wandered and wavered, I believe I will need to forgive myself for not putting my complete trust in God and just continue with my journey. This experience has only strengthened my outlook on the chosen few in the Bible that were tested and tried, but somehow had the strength to completely submit their lives over to God. I know there will be times when I will continue to wish I had not failed, but maybe forgiving and finally forgetting will help with this struggle. And if someone close to you has chosen to take his or her life, I hope you will find hope in Jesus and see the other set of footprints that are in the sand next to yours.

28 Visit a funeral home

31 make a bad t ugh

32 facing the room

41 let go, let God

44 120 mile bike ride

45 God constant companion

56 I don't speak Russian :)

67 Something 2 need to walk
     through.

70 Anything good can become an
     idol when your desire for it
     becomes a demand.

72 Dark "night of the soul" ?

72 Count Blessings per mom

74 Praying for others that are
     causing you angst !

76 Patience a virtue

79 The life we each lead has
     always been a journey.

80 Reincarnation no ....
     followed by Red Dog story :)

81 5's early church regarded
     suicide a sin to spend your
     days in hell !

82 Enjoying simple pleasures of
     life after college,

83 cliff jumping   Daredevil ! :)

84 response to friends question
     if Brother went to heaven?

87 Boy Scout merit badge 7th grade
     night alone in woods ;

95 letter to kids

CPSIA information can be obtained
at www.ICGtesting.com
Printed in the USA
JSHW031529140621
15877JS00001B/6

9 781977 240255

96 Turn the reins over t
     enjoy the ride.